SO-AJC-251

THE POLITICS OF HOSTILITY

THE POLITICS OF HOSTILITY

CASTRO'S REVOLUTION AND UNITED STATES POLICY

BY

LYNN DARRELL BENDER

PUBLISHED BY

INTER AMERICAN UNIVERSITY PRESS

HATO REY, PUERTO RICO 00919

1975

For information write

Inter American University Press
Box 1293
Hato Rey, Puerto Rico 00919

Cover design by Creative Group
Library of Congress Catalog Card Number 74-78314
ISBN 0-913-480-24-X HC
ISBN 0-913-480-27-4 PB
First printing
Printed in Spain
Impreso en España
Depósito legal B. 1.717 - 1975
Impreso por Grafimar, S. A.
Rocafort, 152 - Barcelona (España)

TABLE OF CONTENTS

For my parents,
Laurence, Andrew and
Guillermo A. Naveiro (R.I.P.)

To live a full life
a man must have a son,
plant a tree, and write
a book.

(Chinese proverb)

Acknowledgments

This book is old-fashioned in the sense that it represents a one-man effort—with all the defects which this limitation is bound to incur. It would never have reached this state, however, without the encouragement, support, and assistance of many others.

The core of this work comprises the doctoral dissertation which I prepared at the George Washington University, an institution that provided me with considerable material support throughout my graduate studies. It was also at George Washington where I had the privilege to study and work with (not under) Professor Ralph E. Purcell. I am indebted to him for implanting in me a requisite dosis of self-confidence at the crucial moment of moving into a new career field. Moreover, as my mentor, I am grateful for a close association with an eminently human political scientist. His own instincts and political passions were a strong influence, encouraging me to resist the path taken by so many of my contemporaries who attempt to remove the perplexity, the uncertainty, and the fun from the study of politics.

I am also very pleased with the expressions of encouragement that I have received from my colleagues and the administration of the Inter American University. In particular, I am thankful for the monetary support provided by the *Caribbean Institute and Study Center for Latin America* (CISCLA) at our San Germán campus. And, I am certainly compelled to add a note of gratitude to the staff of the Inter American University Press—to John Zebrowski, its director-editor, for his sympathetic cooperation, and to Richard Hall who, during his temporary association with the Press, did a superb editing job on my manuscript.

Lastly, I thank the editors and publishers of several professional and academic journals for permission to incorporate into this book the following articles adapted from the original manuscript:

"U. S. Cuban Policy: Subtle Modifications and the Implications of the American-Soviet 'Understandings,'" *The Journal of International and Comparative Studies* (now *Potomac Review*), Vol. 5, No. 2 (Spring 1972), pp. 50-67.

"U. S. Cuban Policy Under the Nixon Administration: Subtle Modifications," *Revista/Review Interamericana*, Vol. II., No. 3 (Fall 1972), pp. 330-341.

"Guantánamo: Its Political, Military and Legal Status," *Caribbean Quarterly*, Vol. 19, No. 1 (March 1973), pp. 80-86.

"U. S. Claims Against the Cuban Government: An Obstacle to Rapprochement," *Inter-American Economic Affairs*, Vol. 27, No. 1 (Summer 1973), pp. 3-13.

"The Cuban Exiles: An Analytical Sketch," *Journal of Latin American Studies* (London), Vol. 5, Part 2 (November 1973), pp. 271-278.

"Gitmo: Vestige of Americana in Cuba," United States Naval Institute *Proceedings*, Vol. 99, No. 12/850 (December 1973), pp. 114-116.

"Cuba, the United States, and Sugar," *Caribbean Studies*, Vol. 14, No. 1 (April 1974).

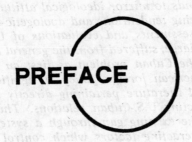

PREFACE

Somehow the Cuban revolution has survived 15 long and tumultuous years of historical existence. From the very beginning, its impact has stirred emotions, challenged assumptions, and resisted generalizations. In fact, no final judgment can yet be rendered on the revolutionary process; its essence, implications, and progression remain largely a mystery.

Since even before the successful installation of the revolutionary regime in 1959, there has been a veritable outpouring of literature on all aspects of the revolution.[1] Most striking, however, is the paucity of objective and well-documented information, a characteristic which has tended to distort American perceptions of today's Cuba. Nevertheless, the lack of hard, verified facts on conditions and developments in Cuba itself should be seen as a distressing yet understandable phenomenon, given the inevitable confusion present in a revolutionary setting.[2] And the difficulty is further compounded by political obstacles that have curtailed on-site scholarly research.[3] The object of these introductory comments is, therefore, to justify still another

1. For evidence of the vastness of extant literature on revolutionary Cuba, see Nelson P. Valdés and Edwin Lieuwen, *The Cuban Revolution: a Research-Study Guide (1959-1969)*, (Albuquerque: University of New Mexico Press, 1971); Jaime Suchlicki, *The Cuban Revolution: A Documentary Guide, 1952-1969* (Coral Gables: University of Maimi Press, 1971); and Gilberto V. Fort, *The Cuban Revolution of Fidel Castro Viewed From Abroad: An Annotated Bibliography* (Laurence: University of Kansas Libraries, 1969).

2. Carmelo Mesa-Lago, a scholar of Cuban origin, explores certain aspects of this problem in "Availability and Reliability of Statistics in Socialist Cuba," *Latin American Research Review* (Spring 1969), pp. 53-91; (Fall 1969), pp. 47-81.

3. The best known of the empirically-based studies on Cuba, now dated, are Maurice Zeitlin, *Revolutionary Politics and the Cuban Working Class* (Princeton, N. J.: Princeton University Press, 1967), and Dudley Seers, *et al., Cuba, The Eco-*

contribution to the literary inundation on Cuban themes by explaining this study's purpose, scope, and basic conclusions.

The passions unleashed by the Cuban revolution have produced a literature which tends to mirror ideological attitudes. It can thus be characterized as being tendentious and apologetic—in a word, highly positional. The assessments and evaluations of U.S. policy toward Cuba have, by and large, suffered from the general trend. And, despite the centrality of the Cuban problem as first an active and now a latent issue in American foreign policy, a significant lacuna exists in regard to useful literature pertaining directly to the core issues and obstacles affecting U.S.-Cuban relations.[4] This study attempts, therefore, to fill the existing gap through a systematic and critical analysis of the interacting factors which control American foreign policy in its Cuban context.

The focus of the study deliberately centers on the U.S.-Cuban relationship as an American foreign policy problem. In all studies of this nature, the conceptual boundary between the national and international systems becomes blurred; in the process of locating basic causes, it is soon discovered that most variables interweave the two systems. Thus, although considerable effort is made to weigh the domestic sources for U.S. policy attitudes and practices toward Cuba, by necessity certain attention must be given to the goals, interests, and perspectives of Cuba. And, to complicate the analytic scheme, similar factors in terms of the Soviet Union must also be considered. In short, the analytical framework seeks to accommodate the strands of an entangled triangular international relationship.

It is also important to note that the study postulates a conceptual model for the existing U.S.-Cuban relationship based on the idea of "mutual hostility." Central to this concept is the proposition that the mutual distrust between the two countries developed from an intense reactive process, during which each side believed its hostility was a justified reaction to the hostile actions of the other. Once this basic hostile orientation was established, the adversary relationship became self-perpetuating as the behavior of one side only served to make its threat-image appear more genuine to the other. The basis for the

nomic and Social Revolution (Chapel Hill: University of North Carolina Press, 1964).

4. Richard R. Fagen, an academic with outstanding credentials, has written extensively on Cuban political themes. Among his writings is a highly useful monograph dealing with the contextual elements of America's Cuban policy: "United States-Cuban Relations," in David S. Smith, ed., Prospects for Latin America, The International Fellows Program Series (N. Y.: Columbia University, 1970).

initial attitudes was not, however, only psychological; the perceptions of fear or threat had a foundation in reality. What emerged, nonetheless, was a set of attitudes that has resulted in a gradually hardened public policy position. Moreover, having once been firmly fixed, the mutual threat-image has been sustained by a vicious circle of seemingly intransigent hostility. The fact is, however, that the intensity of this hostility has varied over time, and today is riding along on its own momentum.

No political accommodation between the United States and Cuba can take place until the long-sustained adversary relationship is, in some manner, fundamentally modified. A good example of a similarly patterned relationship was that of the U.S.-Communist China antagonism, which now has seemingly been altered as a consequence of a new spirit of accommodation evidenced by both parties. The prospects for a corresponding U.S.-Cuban rapprochement are discussed in this study. Here the problem is more complex, complicated by the intimate geographic, historical, and political associations which had tied Cuba and the United States together for decades prior to the Castro epoch and compounded by the virulence and intense acrimony that characterized relations between the two governments, particularly during the crucial 1959-1960 period.

This study outlines how U.S. Cuban policy itself has evolved through six historical phases, characterized principally by a course of action reminiscent of the post-World War II containment policy. Although ostensibly designed to stop the Castro contagion in Latin America, the policy held out hopes—at least during the initial stages—of actually choking off the Castro regime through political and economic suffocation. Evidence now suggests that the early removal of the Castro regime is now no longer viewed as attainable, nor particularly essential for U.S. interests. Yet, publicly the same policy persists. There has been, therefore, a change in attitudes without a corresponding modification in supportive policy actions.

The study further stresses that the principal objection to present U.S. Cuban policy is its lack of flexibility for dealing with the long-range implications of Cuba from the standpoint of strategic interests and future regional relationships. Even a minimal breakthrough in communications would tend to give U.S. policy makers increased maneuverability. There is also the consideration that the present policy strategy is actually counterproductive: it encourages closer Soviet-Cuban ties and the continuation of Cuban behaviors which the United States regards highly objectionable.

The analysis examines various alternatives available to the United States should reciprocal actions open the door to a transformation of policy, as well as several obstacles that stand in the way of its attainment. It emphasizes that discernible trends strongly suggest the availability of only two alternatives open to the United States at this time: (1) the continuation of the current "low-intensity" containment policy strategy or (2) the adoption of an accommodative policy strategy whose goals would be to seek actively—but prudently and gradually— the eventual "regularization" of relations with the Castro regime.

Policy studies on contemporary issues tend to be highly subjective even when the researcher has free and total access to key decision makers and the foreign policy decision-making machinery of all parties involved. When there is an absence of direct personal experience or access to confidential intelligence reports, an estimate of Cuban realities must be reached, primarily, on the basis of freely available information. The most important are written materials, for these can more easily be scrutinized and compared for consistency and probable veracity. It must be admitted, nevertheless, that many of the judgments expressed in this study are non-verifiable and open to debate.

Another source of information can be opinions expressed by experts, participants, and key policy makers in private interview situations. Interviews of this type provided the writer with insights not found in written documents. Some of these insights have been passed on unattributed, but only to conform to specific requests for anonymity. Therefore, much of the analysis based on the information supplied by these persons can in no way be verified, even indirectly through institutional identification. This, of course, is a problem in all research conducted on pending foreign relations issues and one to be resolved by each researcher individually.

Furthermore, to a considerable extent, this study is derivational, in that it attempts to synthesize viewpoints and data found in already published materials. Although some may view such an effort disparagingly, in this case, given the vastness of the extant literature, the very bringing together of a multitude of opinions and findings may equally be seen as a timely and useful labor. In any event, the writer is not absolved from taking the responsibility for all analyses and judgments rendered in this study, which are his alone.

Most of the research and writing for this study took place during 1971-1972. Little has been done to modify the original text, since subsequent events have tended to confirm or affect only slightly my prior analyses and judgments. Pertinent developments occurring later are analyzed in the final chapter.

L. D. B.
San Germán, Puerto Rico

CHAPTER 1

BACKGROUND: THE TRADITIONAL LINKS OF THE U.S.-CUBAN RELATIONSHIP

For the United States, the projection of a Cuban threat-image, so vivid during the early 1960's, has receded to a rather remote corner of the nation's awareness. What persists, however, is a heavy residue of the anger, bitterness, and hostility that characterized even the earliest United States encounters with the Cuban revolutionaries in power. Moreover, the continuing adversary relationship has taken on seemingly implacable attributes. This study attempts to trace the contours, the implications, and the consequences of this relationship. To begin, it may be helpful to visualize the acrimony as a product of estrangement, a sharp break with the past. Forming the core of this past are two basic elements: (1) geography and (2) historical sentiment. Ironically, besides defining the intimacy of the traditional U.S.-Cuban ties, these same factors also account, in part, for the origins of the Cuban revolution.[1]

1. For their emphasis on the historical precedents of the U. S.-Cuban relationship, particularly useful works to consult are: Hugh Thomas' massive tome *Cuba: The Pursuit of Freedom* (New York: Harper & Row, 1971); an article by the same author, "The Origins of the Cuban Revolution," *The World Today*, 19 (October 1963); Lester D. Langley, *The Cuban Policy of the United States: A Brief History* (New York: John Wiley & Sons, Inc., 1968); Wyatt MacGaffey and Clifford

1

The United States, Cuba, and the Caribbean: Geographic Fatalism[2]

Geographical propinquity alone would give the United States a legitimate interest in the Caribbean. And, indeed, since it became the paramount power in the hemisphere around the turn of the century, this country's involvement in the area has been extraordinary. In strictly foreign policy terms, however, the Caribbean today is scarcely perceived as an immediate problem area for the United States. In fact, for most Americans, even those deeply engrossed in questions pertaining to the country's foreign relations, the Caribbean—including Cuba—remains politically unknown.

The evanescent qualities of historical memory and the nation's pressing problems in other areas of the world have combined to make Americans forget the extent to which their nation's past foreign policy was consumed with Caribbean questions. To paraphrase one American historian, it would be well to remember that present American foreign policy attitudes were, in significant measure, hammered out on the Caribbean anvil.[3] Indelibly persisting, however, is the legacy of U.S. activity and presence, the experiences of which remain deeply embedded in the fabric of the Caribbean national consciousness.

Inasmuch as all the countries of the area are small and weak, it was perhaps inevitable that the vitality and boisterousness of America's dynamism would first overflow to engulf these neighboring states. Although some were nominally independent and sovereign, none could escape the commercial and economic weight of the "Colossus of the North." Moreover, they soon learned that political penetration closely followed on the heels of unrestricted economic penetration—and, in some cases, actual physical intervention. No other geographic area, even today, is subject to the full range and intensity of American power and influence as is the Caribbean. For decades, the United States has treated the area as vital to its national security and one from which all hostile powers are to be excluded.

R. Barnett, *Twentieth Century Cuba: Background of the Cuban Revolution* (Garden City, N. J.: Doubleday Anchor, 1965); Ramón Eduardo Ruiz, *Cuba: The Making of a Revolution* (New York: W. W. Norton & Co., 1970); and a classic of Cuban historiography, Herminio Portell Vila, *Historia de Cuba en sus relaciones con los Estados Unidos y España* (Havana: Jesus Montero, 1939-1941).

2. Herbert S. Dinerstein uses this term in "Soviet Policy in Latin America," *American Political Science Review*, 61:1 (March 1967), p. 84.

3. Frank Tannenbaum, *Mexico: The Struggle for Peace and Bread* (London: Jonathan Cape, 1950), p. 253.

As the nearest Caribbean island nation to the United States—and the largest and richest of the Antilles—Cuba experienced and suffered the consequences of its geographic proximity. More so, in fact, than most of the other countries. In purely geopolitical terms, control of Cuba was perceived by Americans as vital to U.S. national security, particularly from the viewpoint of naval strategy. For years American attitudes were conditioned to view Cuba through the eyes of the famed naval strategist Alfred Thayer Mahan, who wrote: "Cuba is surely the key to the Gulf of Mexico as Gibraltar is to the Mediterranean." [4] It was assumed that a hostile Cuba would pose a strategic threat to the United States.

Even today many continue to underscore the crucial role of Cuba in relation to U.S. "control" of the Caribbean on the basis of the same geopolitical perspective. Writings and congressional testimony by military spokesmen on security questions related to the Caribbean, Cuba, and the Panama Canal frequently reiterate the same well-worn—and largely obsolete—geopolitical arguments. The following can be considered standard strategic thinking:

> Our concern there is not only the transmission of an ideology among the islands of the Caribbean and the countries around it, but with the role Cuba could play in disrupting our lines of communications through the Caribbean, as well as lines to Europe and Asia through the sea passages and the Panama Canal—the disrupting of our support to and from Latin America. [5]

Just how Castro—or the Soviet Union for that matter—could, in fact, "disrupt" U. S. lines of communication through the area is never explained. Any endeavor, such as attempts to stop the free passage of ships, would unquestionably call forth the full weight of America's overbearing military strength in the region.

The standard geopolitical perspectives relative to the Caribbean are, of course, only marginally relevant in this modern age of nuclear weapons, atomic submarines, and intercontinental missiles. Today, all potential military targets are vulnerable and security is enhanced only slightly by the factor of distance. It is, moreover, considered highly improbable that the superpowers would or could engage in any protracted conventional warfare; thus, the importance of retaining a capa-

4. Quoted in Arthur M. Wilcox, "Cuba's Place in U. S. Naval Strategy," *U. S. Naval Institute Proceedings*, Vol. 88, No. 12 (December 1962), p. 39.
5. Roland H. del Mar (retired Major General, former director of the Inter-American Defense College), "Strategic Characteristics of the Caribbean," A. Curtis Wilgus, ed., *The Caribbean: Its Hemispheric Role* (Gainesville: University of Florida Press, 1967), p. 157.

city to keep sea passages open for communication lines and essential trade is correspondingly diminished.

Nonetheless, today with the intromission of cold war politics and power into the Caribbean through Cuba, the salience of a Cuban threat continues to be perceived by the American public and the country's political leadership. And perceptions of this nature, whether real or imagined, remain decisive in political terms so long as they are believed. The geographic proximity of a hostile Cuba to the United States has thus added considerably to the Castro threat-image.[6]

Paternalistic Clientage

Besides the special strategic importance which the United States has traditionally attached to Cuba, it has further maintained, for decades, a sentimental relationship that transcends national security considerations. Before Castro, this relationship had involved the United States deeply in Cuban internal affairs. Developing over decades, a pattern of American interference in and dominance over the political and economic destinies of Cuba became very much a way of life —much to the displeasure of some vocal Cuban patriots. The process of this envelopment in its early stages is succinctly described by a well-known American historian:

> It was no wonder the Spaniards expected the United States to annex Cuba. Jefferson had included it as part of his dream of expansion; John Quincy Adams considered it indispensable to the continuance and integrity of the Union; the South coveted it; Polk tried to purchase it; and the Ostend Manifesto prepared to steal it.[7]

Following the Spanish-American War of 1898, when Cuba became a direct American responsibility, a highly sophisticated political compromise between full annexation and independence provided a semi-protectorate status for Cuba. It allowed for U. S. control of the island without the administrative problems inherent in the traditional

6. An interesting public opinion survey seems to support this statement. The following question was asked in a nationwide survey conducted in December 1967:
"Which country do you regard as the greater threat to the United States —a communist-controlled Cuba or a communist-controlled Vietnam?"

Cuba	43 percent
Vietnam	42 percent
No opinion	15 percent

(from *Polls*, Vol. III, No. 4 (1968), p. 76).

7. Charles S. Olcott, *The Life of William McKinley*, Vol. II (Boston: Houghton Mifflin Co., 1916), p. 195.

colonial pattern based on actual physical occupation. The instrument to achieve this dominance was the infamous Platt Amendment, named after its sponsor Senator Orville Platt of Connecticut. Attached first to the Army appropriation bill in 1901, it was subsequently written into a 1904 treaty with Cuba and incorporated into Cuba's first republican constitution.[8] The United States intervened directly in Cuba three times under its provisions. The amendment was finally abrogated by President Franklin D. Roosevelt in 1934 as an expression of his administration's "Good Neighbor" policy toward Latin America.

8. The more significant clauses of the amendment, whose effects so significantly vitiated U. S.-Cuban relations, are:

(1) That the Government of Cuba shall never enter into any treaty or other compact with any foreign Power or Powers which will impair or tend to impair the independence of Cuba, nor in any manner authorize or permit any foreign Power or Powers to obtain by colonization or for military or naval purposes, or otherwise, lodgment in or control over any portion of said Island.

(2) That said Government shall not assume or contract any public debt to pay the interest upon which, and to make reasonable sinking-fund provisions for discharge of which, the ordinary revenues of the Island, after defraying the current expenses of the Government, shall be inadequate.

(3) That the Government of Cuba consents that the United States may exercise the right to intervene for the preservation of Cuban independence, the maintenance of a government adequate for the protection of life, property, and individual liberty, and for discharging the obligations with respect to Cuba imposed by the Treaty of Paris on the United States, now to be assumed and undertaken by the Government of Cuba.

(4) That all acts of the United States in Cuba during its military occupation thereof are ratified and validated, and all lawful rights acquired thereunder shall be maintained and protected.

(5) That the Government of Cuba will execute, and as far as necessary extend, the plans already devised or other plans to be mutually agreed upon, for the sanitation of the cities of the Island to the end that a recurrence of epidemic and infectious diseases may be prevented, thereby assuring protection to the people and commerce of Cuba, as well as to the commerce of the Southern ports of the United States and the people residing therein.

(6) That the Isle of Pines shall be omitted from the proposed constitutional boundaries of Cuba, the title thereto left to future adjustments by treaty.

(7) That to enable the United States to maintain the independence of Cuba, and to protect the people thereof, as well as for its own defense, the Government of Cuba will sell or lease to the United States lands necessary for coaling or naval stations at certain specified points, to be agreed upon with the President of the United States.

(8) That by way of further assurance the Government of Cuba will embody the foregoing provisions in a permanent treaty with the United States.

(See Graham H. Stuart, *Latin America and the United States* [5th ed.; New York: Appleton-Century-Crofts, 1955], pp. 213-214.)

By the 1930's, however, U. S. tutelage had been well established. American dominance continued on a *de facto* basis by virtue of the overwhelming presence in the Cuban economy of U. S. capital, citizens, and interests—most often with the collaboration, participation, and assistance of large numbers of middle and upper-class Cubans. The island's economy was virtually in a colonial status vis-à-vis the United States. By 1940, even *Business Week*, a conservative American publication, candidly reported that "politically and economically, Cuba is an adjunct of the United States".[9] And in 1956, just prior to the time Castro and his rebel band became engaged in guerrilla warfare in the Sierra Maestra Mountains, a U. S. Department of Commerce survey observed:

> The only foreign investments of importance are those of the United States. American participation exceeds 90 percent of telephone and electric services, about 50 percent in public service railways, and roughly 40 percent in raw sugar production. The Cuban branches of U. S. banks are entrusted with about one-fourth of all bank deposits. This intimate economic relation is so much the outgrowth of mutual helpful assistance that many of the problems that have plagued less close relationships in other areas have largely been avoided in Cuba.[10]

It is tempting to overstate the case of U. S. economic dominance in Cuba, but certain crucial facts cannot be dismissed. U. S. direct investment was large—in fact, its book value was greater than anywhere in Latin America except Venezuela.[11] *Certified* claims against the Castro government for nationalized U. S. properties total $ 1.8 billion, but these same claimants have asserted that the actual value of their total property holdings was $ 3.35 billion.[12] In either case, the amount is substantial. But, perhaps even more significant was the overtness or visibility of the over-all U. S. economic presence in Cuba: U. S. products, advertising, automobiles, machinery, and business techniques were by far predominant; two-thirds of the U. S. direct investment was concentrated in large, non-competitive public utilities; U. S. firms still directly controlled 40 percent of the sugar production; and seven of Cuba's ten largest land holdings were Ameri-

9. Quoted in Langley, *Cuban Policy...*, p. 164.
10. U. S. Department of Commerce, Bureau of Foreign Commerce, *Investment in Cuba: Basic Information for U. S. Businessmen* (Washington: Government Printing Office, 1956), p. 10.
11. Leland C. Johnson, "U. S. Business Interests in Cuba and the Rise of Castro," *World Politics*, Vol. XVII, No. 3 (April 1965), p. 440.
12. See Chapter VIII for a detailed discussion of U. S. claims against the Cuban government.

can controlled.[13] And, finally, the sale of its sugar production—the most decisive economic factor, and the one upon which the nation's total economic performance hinged—depended directly on decisions made by the United States.

Despite the purported mutuality of benefits stemming from the neo-colonial economic arrangement,[14] behind the facade of prosperity and well-being were chronic and serious imbalances in the Cuban economy, traditional corruption and graft in government, and historic political instability. All of these factors, when added to the dependency status,[15] exacerbated the feeling of frustration and instilled a degrading psychological subordination to the United States. The vast majority of Cubans, like most citizens in all countries, accepted life as it was. But once the prevailing situation changed sharply, it took no great effort on the part of the revolutionary leadership to convince the Cuban masses that the United States had infringed on Cuba's national sovereignty. Thus, the United States became an easy target and the Cuban revolutionaries' principal enemy.

The Challenge of Fidelismo

Fidel Castro was not Cuba's first revolutionary or military hero. His appearance at a decisive historic moment—aided by his stamina, courage, tenacity, undaunted optimism, almost mystical magnetism, and plenty of good fortune—did, however, crystallize the revolutionary dynamics and forces which had long been fermenting. The rule of Fulgencio Batista, who had been the strongman in Cuban politics since 1934 (interrupted only during 1944-1952), by 1958 had become too oppressive. Castro, fighting in the remote areas of Cuba since his return to the island in 1956,[16] led a small band of guerrilla forces that

13. Johnson, "U. S. Business Interests...," pp. 450-452.

14. Compared with other Latin American nations, Cuba ranked fairly high on several socio-economic indices in the late 50's, such as literacy (5th), number of television sets per capita (1st), number of inhabitants per physician (3rd), gross national product per capita (4th), etc. See Richard R. Fagen, "Revolution: For Internal Consumption Only," Irving Louis Horowitz, *Cuban Communism* (New York: Aldine Publishing Co., 1970), p. 41.

15. Considering only trade relations, Cuba was highly dependent upon the U. S. In 1958, for example, 66 percent of its exports ($ 527.8 million) went to and 70 percent of its imports ($ 546.9 million) came from the United States. See The Cuban Economic Research Project, *A Study on Cuba* (Coral Gables, Florida: University of Miami Press, 1965.) Today, however, Cuba's trade dependency on the Soviet Union is even higher in percentage terms.

16. Castro had been captured, tried, and jailed after leading an heroic though senseless and abortive assault on the Moncada army barracks in 1953. It was

never really defeated the Batista dictatorship militarily; the latter's forces and following merely crumbled and collapsed demoralized.

Castro and his followers easily slipped into the vacuum created by Batista's hasty departure on December 31, 1958. They rode the high tide of massive public support while the traditional middle-class political forces became immobilized, indecisive, and eventually irremediably fragmented. Castro had led a revolutionary movement that was neither bourgeois, peasant, nor proletarian in composition and leadership. It represented, rather, a force headed by *déclassé* young intellectuals—elements of the middle-class themselves—who had fought in the name of peasants and workers without a party organization or a defined ideology.[17] Castro himself, as undisputed "maximum leader," provided the charismatic leadership and inspiration to sustain national cohesion and a revolutionary *élan* throughout his chameleonic progression from an anti-communist, anti-capitalist "constitutional democrat" to a "humanist," a "socialist," a "Marxist-Leninist," and then, finally, as a "communist."[18] The radicalization of the revolution, it is important to keep in mind, took place not as a result of a clearly conceived plan, but by virtue of "an interplay of spontaneous decisions made by the leader."[19]

Most analysts have by now concluded that Cuba's "old-line" communists played a minimal and weak role in the unfolding of the revolutionary process;[20] they are, likewise, fully in accord in viewing

---

during his trial that he delivered his now famous "History Will Absolve Me" speech. Released under a general amnesty proclamation, he proceeded to Mexico where he met "Che" Guevara, and with assistance from various sources, trained a small band of followers, only a few of whom escaped a Batista trap awaiting them when they returned to Cuba in 1956 aboard the boat "Granma." Those who had escaped, including Fidel, his brother Raúl, and "Che" Guevara, formed the nucleus of the guerrilla force that eventually propelled itself into power.

17. These and the following comments on the Cuban revolution, its nature, its progression, and the role of the revolutionary leadership, draw heavily on Theodore Draper's two books, *Castro's Revolution: Myths and Realities* (New York: Thomas and Hudson, 1962) and *Castroism: Theory and Practice* (New York: Praeger, 1965), as well as Boris Goldenberg, *The Cuban Revolution and Latin America* (New York: Praeger, 1965).

18. For a full analysis of the ideological facets underpinning the Cuban revolution in its many phases, see Loree Wilkerson, *Fidel Castro's Political Programs from Reformism to Marxism-Leninism* (Gainesville: University of Florida Press, 1965) and Andrés Suárez, *Cuba: Castroism and Communism, 1959-1966* (Cambridge, Mass.: M. I. T. Press, 1967).

19. Goldenberg, *op. cit.*, p. 40.

20. American socialists Leo Huberman and Paul M. Sweezy (see their *Cuba: Anatomy of a Revolution*, New York: Monthly Review Press, 1961) were among the first to see the Cuban revolutionary experience as being the first socialist revolution not organized by communists.

Castro as the central figure and the fountainhead of revolutionary inspiration. Some observers see Castro's desire to monopolize power as the consideration which motivated and propelled him to move the revolution toward communism and association with the socialist camp.[21] This is plausible, but his devotion to a cause—the duty to break Cuba permanently away from what he may have viewed as an intolerable political, social, and economic structure and dependency relationship with the United States—would have also taken him along the same path. And, due to the contemporary international power configuration, this path leads to the same ideological and political camp. Such points, of course, will long be debated. There are yet many pieces to add to the gaping holes in the giant Cuban puzzle.

Fidelismo was directed against the United States, not in the sense of a direct physical threat, but as the embodiment of a political influence, continental in scope. It openly and raucously defied the continent's hegemonial power and the latter's goals and objectives in the Western Hemisphere—the desire (1) to keep the area quiescent, (2) to keep communism and Soviet influence there at a minimum, and (3) to retain the power patterns inherent in a basically sphere-of-influence conceptualization of hemispheric politics. The challenge became manifest as the revolutionary regime quickly moved to end the U.S.'s privileged position in Cuban affairs. This, in part, explains the bitterness of the ensuing mutually-reactive, U.S.-Cuban hostility which marked relations between the two countries during the critical first months of the Castro regime—and up to the present day.

As noted, geography, historical sentiment, and excessive political and economic involvement created an "intimacy" between Cuba and the United States which contained the seeds of conflict. From the Cuban side, hostility was generated by (1) the revolutionary regime's deliberate and vociferous casting aside of the U.S.'s paternalistic ties with Cuba, which it viewed as tantamount to imperialistic bondage (2) Castro's feeling that U. S. public opinion and leadership would not tolerate the measures that he deemed had to be taken to carry out a throughgoing revolution in Cuba and (3) alleged counter-revolutionary acts perpetrated by the U.S. government. Hostility on the part of the United States, in contrast, emanated from (1) hurt and anger directed against Cuba's rejection of the traditional U.S.-Cuban relationship [22] (2) U.S. moralizing denunciations of the revo-

21. See, in particular, Andrés Suárez, *op. cit., passim.*
22. Apropos of the traditional U. S.-Cuban relationship, historian Lester D. Langley remarks:

9

lution's "excesses" during the first months of 1959, based on the regime's political executions and its massive expropriations of U.S. properties and (3) a deep-seated concern based on the undisputed fact that for the first time a hostile regime closely associated with a strong, extracontinental, rival power was firmly situated only ninety miles from the U. S.'s exposed and strategically vital southern flank.

Fifteen years under one regime is a long time in the historical development of any country. Unquestionably, the societal and structural changes which have taken place in Cuba during this period will have profound implications for future U. S. policies. The U. S. hope for a Cuban *status quo ante* with democracy may well have been a viable prospect until, perhaps, 1962, but one must question the possibility, or indeed the desirability, of such an eventuality after this now lengthy period of major socio-economic transformation. For a long period U. S. policy toward Cuba was aimed at sanitizing the Americas from "communist" Cuba's pernicious influences. The hope was that a containment policy could bring Cuba to its knees, mar its value as a model for other under-developed countries, and, perhaps, lead in some way to the downfall of the revolution's driving force—Fidel Castro.

Although the basic policy framework remains intact today, the goals sought by U. S. Cuban policy have become more ambiguous. The United States is now seemingly convinced that a regime of the Castro type may well be a permanent fixture of the Cuban political environment. Moreover, it is apparently no longer certain that the situation which might emerge from a Castro-less vacuum would, in fact, be more desirable. Whatever the case, U. S. policy makers and interested American citizens must ponder such questions if present policies are to be shaped toward desirable future outcomes. U. S. Cuban policy, therefore, seems to merit at this time a fresh assessment and evaluation.

"It is not Castro's political dictatorship that is so repulsive as his open denial of the Jacksonian credos of democracy, capitalism, and progress. For that reason alone there will probably be no reconciliation with Cuba as long as Castro is in power... But resumption of Cuban-U. S. harmony will mean necessarily the rejection of much of the nineteenth century view about Cuba..."
(from Langley, *The Cuban Policy...*, p. 187.)

PART I

SURVEYING
THE AMERICAN
PERSPECTIVE

CHAPTER II

THE EVOLUTION OF U.S. POLICY TOWARD THE CUBAN REVOLUTIONARY REGIME

Amid the wild jubilation, enthusiasm, and euphoria of the Cuban revolutionaries' first months in power, actions and events began to define the radical political orientation of the Castro regime. Moving through progressive stages, each twist downward toward a more profound radicalization of the revolutionary process cut away at the core elements which had formed the traditional U. S.-Cuban relationship. Whatever interpretation given to account for the reasons, motives, and events which determined the radical course of the revolution,[1]

1. On this point, James O'Connor (*The Origins of Socialism in Cuba* [Ithaca, N. Y.: Cornell University Press, 1969]) has divided extant literature into four contending schools of thought: (1) the "Revolution Betrayed" thesis reflects the official U. S. position in the early 60's, underscoring Castro's drive for personal power as the factor that accounts for his "betrayal" of the nationalistic, democratic ideals and goals he had supported before 1959 (see Theodore Draper, *Castro's Revolution: Myths and Realities* [N. Y.: Thomas and Hudson, 1962]; and *Castroism: Theory and Practice* [N. Y.: Praeger, 1965]); (2) the "Communist Conspiracy" thesis represents the extreme right view that Castro was always a communist agent, and that he delivered Cuba to the Russians (see Daniel James, *Cuba, The First Soviet Satellite in the Americas* [N.Y.: Avon Books, 1961]; and Nathaniel Weyl, *Red Star Over Cuba* [N. Y.: Devin-Adair, Co., 1960]); (3) the "U. S. Opposition", thesis emphasizes that Castro was "forced" to the left in

13

the fact remains that a sharp deterioration in relations took place between the two countries.

Intemperate attitudes and policies adopted by the U. S. government and the Castro regime became juxtaposed to produce a "dialectic of hostility." [2] Each government embarked upon a course of action during the crucial 1959-1960 period that ineluctably led to conflict. American officials and the general public were first shocked by the executions of Batista supporters and then alarmed at Cuban provocations directed against American citizens, property, and policies. Thus, an earlier preoccupation turned quickly into near hysteria as Cuba became viewed as the portal for communist and Soviet encroachment into the hemisphere.

The Cubans, too, reacted decisively—and stridently. Castro yoked antagonism toward American political and economic domination to a deliberate decision to direct the energies of the revolution against the *system* and the *agent* which, in his view, had caused the enmiseration of the Cuban people. In short, anti-Americanism conditioned Cuban attitudes. Therefore, American retaliatory actions, such as cutting off the sugar quota and the later economic boycott only served to reinforce the Cuban inclination to attribute past failures and current problems entirely to the United States. Later developments, including the Bay of Pigs invasion, the missile crisis, the Cuban advocacy—and support—of hemispheric subversion, and the regime's increasing network of ties with the Soviet Union, intensified the already well-ingrained mutual hostility pattern.

In broad conceptual terms, then, certain insights can be derived from viewing U. S.-Cuban relations within a framework of mutual

---

the wake of U. S. hostility and intransigent opposition to the revolutionary goals and practices he was espousing (see Maurice Zeitlin and Robert Scheer, *Cuba: Tragedy in Our Hemisphere* [N. Y.: Grove Press, 1963]; William Appleman Williams, *The United States, Cuba, and Castro* [N. Y.: Monthly Review Press, 1962]; and Herbert Matthews, *The Cuban Story* [N. Y.: George Braziller, Inc., 1961]); and (4) O'Connor himself proposes the "Inevitable Socialism" thesis, which advances the view that Cuba's economic transformation was blocked by the very structure of the existing socio-economic and political systems, and that only with a socialist takeover of the political system—with concommitant economic changes—could the country ever hope to achieve sustained economic growth (see also Edward Boorstein, *The Economic Transformation of Cuba* [N. Y.: Monthly Review Press, 1968]). Needless to say, many works combine these various notions in accounting for causation; they, thereby, represent less clear-cut examples of biased, positional literature on this point.

2. The term is taken from Raymond Aron and Alfred Grosser, "A European Perspective," John Plank, ed., *Cuba and the United States: Long-Range Perspectives* (Washington, D. C.: The Brookings Institution, 1967), p. 148.

14

hostility. The reciprocal animosity that underlies this adversary relationship has varied in intensity over time—conditioned by events, attitudes, and personalities. U. S. policy has likewise not remained static, and its passage through several phases can be identified and described. In examining these phases, appropriate emphasis is placed on the mutual hostility setting, tracing through it the origins and the evolutionary contours of American policy toward the Cuban revolutionary regime up to the present day.[3]

Phase I. Seeking Accommodation (January-November 1959)

The U. S. government recognized the newly triumphant revolutionary government of Cuba just seven days after Batista hurriedly and precipitately departed from the island.[4] For the next troublesome and eventful 11 months, in the face of what the Eisenhower administration considered extreme provocations, the U. S. government hoped for the preservation of the basic framework of its traditional (intimate) relationship with Cuba—despite its displeasure with the new Cuban leadership and the latter's nationalistic goals and aspirations. It was initially expected that traditional sentiment and mutual economic advantage would soon subdue revolutionary obstreperousness and enthusiasm. The view was that "constructive"[5] relations would once more contribute to a cooling of passions and bring a measure of stability and moderation to the Cuban internal political environment.

Revolutionary momentum, however, pushed events forward at a rapid pace. In the opening stage, the trials and executions of dozens of ex-Batista collaborators heated American moral sensitivities. Still, the United States believed that the revolution would settle down; after all, the new President, Manuel Urrutia, the Prime Minister, Dr. José Miró Cardona, as well as the rest of the Cabinet were, for the most

3. Particularly valuable here is former Ambassador Philip Bonsal's book *Cuba, Castro, and the United States* (Pittsburgh: University of Pittsburgh Press, 1971). Ambassador Bonsal was the last accredited American ambassador to Cuba, serving there during the Castro regime up to the break in relations on January 3, 1961. Several observations are based on comments made by the Ambassador to this writer in an interview held in November 1971.

4. Batista left Cuba in the late evening of December 31, 1958.

5. See Bonsal, *op. cit., passim.* Throughout his book, Bonsal uses the expressions "constructive", "rational" or "productive" relationships when referring to what he considers thoughtful, sane, or logical policy postures. Most generally, however, he employs them in criticism when referring to Cuba's alleged lack of reasonableness in given adversary contexts.

part, progressive liberals and not wild-eyed, untested, 26-of-July Movement rebels. Castro, however, soon moved to place himself and those who shared his views into key governmental positions. Moreover, as an indication of the revolution's progressive radicalization, Castro was by March already speaking disparagingly about the elections he had "promised" in his earlier *Manifesto of the Sierra Maestra*.[6] He also spoke little of other aspects of constitutional democracy, such as the restoration of the liberal 1940 constitution. The most significant measure, however, was taken on May 17 with the enactment of the basic land reform law. This law, which decisively affected Cuban and vested foreign interests, clearly indicated the type of socio-economic restructuring that the revolutionary regime had in mind.

Meanwhile, inebriated with the ease of their victory over the former dictatorship, the Cuban revolutionaries supported small-scale invasions by exile groups directed at Panama, the Dominican Republic, Haiti, and Nicaragua. In each case the invasions proved futile and abortive. They did, however, lend credence to the Cubans' assertions that they were assuming a leadership role in hemispheric revolution. They also set attitudes—particularly in the United States—which defined the regime as constituting a threat to the security of the Americas. The threat became more believeable as the Castro regime associated itself with the Soviet Union. And, for the first time since the Guatemalan incidents in 1954, cold war politics became a factor of contention in the Western Hemisphere.

During March-April 1959, Castro travelled to the United States. Although invited unofficially, he was the object of considerable curiosity on the part of the general public, and meetings were arranged with high-level American officials. President Eisenhower, nonetheless, decided to give him a cool reception and conveniently removed himself at the time Castro and his entourage arrived in Washington. Castro did speak with Richard Nixon, who was then Vice President. Their private meeting lasted three hours. Nixon later related his impressions of this encounter. His conclusion was: "Castro is either incredibly naive about communism or is under communist discipline."[7] Immediately thereafter, he drafted a memorandum to the Central Intelligence Agency, the State Department, and the White House. His basic recommendation was, instead of "trying to get along with"

6. An "official" pronouncement of Castro's political goals and objectives released on July 12, 1957.

7. Richard Nixon, "Cuba, Castro, and John F. Kennedy," Readers Digest, November 1964, p. 284.

or understanding Castro, that the Cuban revolutionary leader should be removed through the employment of trained exiles.[8] As Karol reminds us, this recommendation was made several weeks before the key land reform law was implemented in Cuba, and at a time when practically all the exiles were Batista men.[9]

Some analysts contend that the U. S. was still in a conciliatory mood at this time, as evidenced by the willingness of American officials to talk about loans and other props for the new government in Cuba. Along with Castro, too, were a number of high-level Cuban economic advisers. But no specific economic talks were held. Castro apparently came around to the notion that the revolution and its goals were fundamentally at odds with continuation of close relations with Washington and the traditional vested interests in Cuba. In this case, then, Castro's refusal to talk economics with the United States was logical. For, after all, it had not been unknown in the past for the United States to use loans, trade, and other financial arrangements in attempts to shape, or even control, Cuba's internal policies.[10] In any event, as a result of this visit, mutual suspicions became more acute.

This phase was to have deep repercussions for the future relationship between both countries. Former U. S. Ambassador Philip W. Bonsal characterizes the American posture at that time as one of "benevolent, if nervous, watchfulness." [11] In effect, the Eisenhower administration's wait-and-see policy toward the Castro regime during the crucial initial period continues to affect official thinking, if only in reverse. The indecisiveness of that phase became to be regarded as an error that could not be repeated. Thus, policy makers have become predisposed to err on the side of overly decisive action rather than risk the emergence of a new Castro-like situation in another strategically sensitive area of the Caribbean. Such considerations underlie the "No Second Cuba" rationale of American policy in the Caribbean. The effects of this thinking became apparent with the unilateral American military intervention in the Dominican Republic in 1965.[12]

8. Richard Nixon, *Six Crises* (N. Y.: Doubleday & Co., 1962), pp. 351-352.
9. K. S. Karol, *Guerrillas in Power: The Course of the Cuban Revolution* (N. Y.: Hill & Wong, 1970), p. 6.
10. See Edward González' article "Castro's Revolution, Cuban Communist Appeals, and the Soviet Response," *World Politics*, Vol. XXI, No. 1 (October 1968), pp. 39-68 for the development and elaboration of this line of analysis. This well-documented and reasoned article has been highly influential and should be considered essential reading for interested students of the Cuban revolution.
11. Bonsal, *Cuba, Castro, and the...*, p. 28.
12. An excellent case study which demonstrates the effects of the "No Second Cuba" policy on the attitudes of key American policy makers is Theodore Draper's *The Dominican Revolt: A Case Study in American Policy* (N. Y.: Comen-

17

At that time, President Lyndon Johnson stated the policy in clear and forceful terms:

> What is important is that we know, and that they know, and that everybody knows, that we don't propose to sit in our rocking chair and let the communists set up any government in the Western Hemisphere.[13]

Uppermost, apparently, in Castro's mind during this initial phase of accelerating conflict with the United States was the historically pertinent example of Guatemala. Castro's perception of the United States was, it now appears, very significantly conditioned by his fear of a repetition in Cuba of the U. S.'s earlier response to the emergence of a "radical" regime in the region.[14] The American actions and reactions to developments in Cuba may well have convinced him, at this early time, that eventually the United States would seek to overthrow the revolutionary regime in Cuba, as it had done in Guatemala—by direct military force, if necessary. If so, this could explain his determination shortly thereafter to seek alternative sources of internal and external support.

Phase II. Formalized Normality (December 1959-February 1960)

This was a short transitional phase in the development of U. S. policy toward the Castro regime. The interactive cycle of mutual hostility continued to compound misunderstandings between the two countries, misunderstandings related, as has been noted, to the already differing expectations and objectives of both governments. Each side virulently denounced the other for its demonstrations of bad faith and illicit behavior. Although a dialogue with the revolutionary leadership had become almost impossible, the United States considered that American interests would be better served by preserving an official diplomatic presence in Cuba.

Thus, the United States maintained the formality of a normal relationship with the revolutionary regime, but now—in contrast to

tary, 1968). See, also, Abraham Lowenthal, *The Dominican Intervention* (Cambridge: Harvard University Press, 1972.)

13. Quoted in Philip L. Geyelin, *Lyndon B. Johnson and the World* (N. Y.: Praeger, 1966), p. 238.

14. For general information and background on U. S. policy in Guatemala at that time, see Ronald Schneider, *Communism in Guatemala, 1944-1954* (N. Y.: Praeger, 1958) and Philip B. Taylor, Jr., "The Guatemalan Affair: A Critique of United States Foreign Policy," *American Political Science Review*, Vol. L, No. 3 (September 1956), pp. 787-806.

the prior phase—with no real conviction that it would be possible to deal realistically with Castro and the revolutionary leadership on fundamental questions affecting American interests.[15] The change in U. S. attitudes was not connected with any one specific Cuban action, but rather resulted from the continuation—and even intensification—of what the U. S. viewed as unwarranted accusations directed against the government of the United States, as well as illegal actions perpetrated against U. S. citizens and interests.

The United States continued its basic "watchful waiting" attitude, but now for a somewhat different reason. Since it was apparent that the Castro regime would not change its revolutionary course to accommodate U. S. interests, American policy makers were now hopeful that internal political pressures would not allow the revolutionary government to hold together. For this reason, the United States believed that a posture of policy drift was preferable to the alternative—immediate, resolute action to remove Castro.

Ambassador Bonsal, for one, believed that inevitably some element would emerge from the growing, but still unorganized, opposition to challenge Castro's leadership and the direction in which he was guiding the revolutionary impulses of the Cuban people.[16] Yet, this same opposition apparently put greater faith for their salvation in the United States—the traditional attitude of Cuba's middle and governing sectors. Bonsal quotes one "representative" Cuban to indicate the prevailing view of the anti-Castro Cubans during this stage:

> We had no confidence in any possible Cuban leadership of the anti-Castro forces, and we did not believe that you, the United States, would let Castro get away with it.[17]

Superficially, however, both governments announced their desire to settle differences amicably. On January 26, 1960, the United States released a statement reaffirming its commitment to non-intervention in Cuban affairs. The document indicated a desire to seek solutions through "appropriate international procedures" while defending the "legitimate" interests of the American government and people.[18] The following day, the Castro government sent a diplomatic note to the United States in which assurances were given that there were no obstacles to negotiations "on the basis of mutual respect and recipro-

15. This analysis draws heavily upon the personal recollections and opinions of Ambassador Bonsal. (Private interview, November 1971.)
16. Bonsal, *Cuba, Castro, and the...*, p. 6.
17. *Ibid.*, p. 6.
18. *Department of State Bulletin*, February 15, 1960, p. 25.

cal benefit." It ended by affirming that the traditional friendship between the two countries was "indestructible." [19] Later, in February, Castro offered to send a commission to Washington to initiate negotiations, but this was rejected by Washington when the Cubans insisted upon a guarantee that the U. S. Congress, in the meantime, would not reduce the Cuban sugar quota.[20] The cycle of mutual recrimination and hostility had already established basic antagonistic attitudes.

Decisive to a further hardening of the antagonism was the visit to Cuba of Soviet First Deputy Premier Anastas Mikoyan, who, on February 15, 1960, signed a trade agreement with the revolutionary regime.[21] This represented the first link in a series of political, economic, and military understandings that progressively tied the destinies of the small and vulnerable Caribbean island to a great power rival of the U. S. Furthermore, it began the basic reorientation of Cuba away from its traditional U. S. relationship. On May 7, 1960, Cuba and Russia re-established full diplomatic relations. With these actions, coupled to the attacks against U. S. property and interests, Castro had overstepped the limits of U. S. toleration, and American policy makers decided that he had to be removed.

Phase III. Toward the Forceful Overthrow of Castro (March 1960-April 1961)

Vice President Nixon's recommendation became a reality when, on March 17, 1960, President Eisenhower ordered that Cuban refugees be organized, trained, and equipped for possible action.[22] And in the ensuing months, threats and counter-threats, actions and counter-actions spiraled U. S.-Cuban relations to their highest plateau of mutual hostility.

Besides the decision to train the exiles for possible action, other

19. Quoted in Martin Kenner and James Petras, *Fidel Castro Speaks* (N. Y.: Grove Press, 1969), p. 36.
20. Bonsal, *Cuba, Castro, and the...*, p. 128.
21. The U. S. S. R. agreed to buy 425,000 tons of Cuba's 1960 sugar harvest plus a million tons for each of the following four years. It also granted a $ 100 million loan at 2.5 percent interest, 20 percent in freely convertible currency and the rest with Soviet goods selected by Cuba at international prices. (See "Joint Communique on Soviet-Cuban Commercial Agreement," February 1960, originally published in *Pravda* (Moscow), February 15, 1960.)
22. Eisenhower divulged this fact on June 12, 1961 at a news conference in Cincinnati, Ohio. Facts on File, *Cuba, the United States and Russia, 1960-1963* (N. Y.: 1964), p. 44. (See also Richard Nixon, "Cuba, Castro, and John F. Kennedy," p. 286.)

deliberate measures were taken with one principal objective in mind —the non-continuation of the Castro regime. These measures were implemented during 1960:[23]

(1) In June, in consultation with high-level government officials, the American and British-owned oil refineries in Cuba refused to process crude oil sent from the Soviet Union. (Cuba retaliated by seizing the installations.)

(2) In July, President Eisenhower announced the "suspension" of the remainder of the Cuban sugar quota for 1960, which amounted to 900,000 tons of the total allocated for all of 1960 (3,119,655 tons), worth approximately $ 92 million. (The Cubans reacted by confiscating a series of properties of U. S. citizens and companies.)

(3) During the same two-month period a coordinated decision was made by the government and the U. S. companies to remove key personnel from American plants in Cuba, a measure designed to put the squeeze on Cuba's productive capacity and output. (Despite disruptions, this technical manpower gap was filled by other Cubans or with imported foreign specialists. By August, the Castro regime had seized all American properties on the island.)

In the meantime, by the summer of 1960 the Eisenhower administration had come to adopt an attitude toward Cuba which significantly shaped events and reactions to events over the next three years: the United States now regarded Castro as an agent of international communism.

By July 1960, in response to Khrushchev's now-famous assertion that "figuratively speaking" the Cuban people would be protected with Soviet rockets, Eisenhower indicated (on July 9) that the United States would uphold its commitments to prevent foreign nations' "interference" in Latin America and would not permit the establishment of a regime dominated by international communism in the Western Hemisphere.[24] And the State Department, in a memorandum to the Inter-American Peace Committee of the Organization of American States (OAS) on August 7, warned that the Cuban government was "now in open league with the Soviet Union and Communist

23. The following is taken directly from Bonsal, *Cuba, Castro, and the United States*, pp. 145-153, supplemented by information provided by the ambassador in the personal interview.
24. Facts on File, *Cuba, the United States, and Russia*, p. 13.

China," and that military relations between the Russians and Cuba constituted the "gravest danger" for the Americas.[25]

On August 25, 1960, the United States pursued a similar anti-Cuban line at the Foreign Ministers' Meeting of the Organization of American States in San José, Costa Rica. Here the United States attempted to get hemispheric support for its position on the basis of a 1954 decision of the organization. That decision had underscored that the states of the region would be threatened if *international communism* were to dominate or control the political institutions of any member state. Despite its efforts, however, the United States obtained only a weak statement of condemnation which spoke about the "threat of intervention" by an extracontinental power without specifically mentioning Cuba.

Nonetheless, the U. S. failure to do something about Castro's Cuba remained very much in the minds of the American public and political leadership. It became an issue in the Kennedy-Nixon presidential campaign in 1960, when Kennedy accused the Republicans of allowing "Castro and his gang" to extinguish freedom in Cuba. In the meantime, the United States officially broke diplomatic relations on January 3, 1961, when the Castro government arbitrarily ordered the U. S. mission to reduce its staff to 18 members within 48 hours. Later, after Kennedy's inauguration, the new administration's spokesmen continued to talk and act along lines similar to those of the preceding Eisenhower administration. For example, in February 1961, Press Secretary Lincoln White commented that the United States was sympathetic with the aims of the revolution, but "concerned with the capture of the revolution by external influences for the purposes of imposing on Cuba an anti-democratic ideology...and exporting that ideology by subversion to other American republics." [26] Kennedy's Cuban policy was, in short, little different in substance from that of Eisenhower—and included the fateful Bay of Pigs invasion plans which he inherited and decided, with reservations, to implement in

---

25. In an earlier memorandum to the same Peace Committee (on June 27, 1960) the State Department alleged:

"The Government of Cuba has for many months conducted an intense campaign of distortions, half-truths, and outright falsehoods against the U. S. Government, its officials, and the people of the United States...the United States has responded to these hostile attitudes with patience and forbearance...the United States Government considers this systematic campaign of hostile propaganda to be offensive and unwarranted."
(from *Department of State Bulletin*, July 18, 1960, pp. 79-86.)

26. Facts on File, *Cuba, the United States, and Russia*, p. 35.

April 1961. This decision led, as is known, to a debacle and a major foreign policy failure.[27]

A series of serious misjudgments made by the principal architects of U. S. foreign policy contributed to the failure to design a policy adequate to accomplish the goal implicit in the actions pursued: to topple the Castro regime in order to prevent the spread of the communist virus in the Western Hemisphere.

Phase IV. *Structuring a Containment Policy (May 1961-1962)*

Following the unsuccessful Bay of Pigs invasion, U. S. Cuban policy entered a new phase. The U. S. government had previously visualized three policy options as alternatives to achieve the goal of ridding Cuba of Castro: (1) invasion using American troops; (2) invasion by exiles (coupled with mass uprisings in Cuba) with U. S. logistic support; (3) economic and political pressures. Option (1) had been rejected from the start and option (2) had been employed with resounding failure. Left, then, with option (3), whose general lines of policy support had already been initiated, the United States embarked on a course of action reminiscent of the post-World War II "containment" policy to arrest what was viewed as communist expansionism. Here, although ostensibly designed to stop the Castro contagion in Latin America, it held out hopes—at least during the initial stage—of actually choking off the Castro regime through political and economic suffocation. This was perceived as a highly desirable goal, particularly after December 1, 1961, when Castro declared himself to be a "Marxist-Leninist."

To implement the new policy line, the United States sought first to isolate Cuba politically. At the Eighth Meeting of Consultation of the Ministers of Foreign Affairs of the Organization of American States, meeting in Punta del Este, Uruguay in January 1962, the United States pressured member states to expel "the present government of Cuba" from the regional organization "by virtue of adherence to Marxism-Leninism and its alignment with the communist bloc..."[28] Doubtful about the legality of the measure, and unsure of American intentions, several of the larger and then more democratic states abstained from the vote. The binding resolution only barely managed

27. A key book on the Bay of Pigs events is Karl E. Meyer and Tad Szulc, *The Cuban Invasion: Chronicle of a Disaster* (N. Y.: Praeger, 1962).

28. For background and texts, see *Department of State Bulletin*, February 19, 1962, p. 270.

to obtain the necessary 14 affirmative votes required for a two-thirds majority. The abstentions were cast by Argentina, Brazil, Chile, Bolivia, Ecuador, and Mexico, which, together, represented two-thirds of Latin America's population.

Then, in a related move on the economic side, the United States unilaterally (on February 3, 1962) imposed a total prohibition on exports to Cuba except for "foodstuffs, medicines, and medical equipment for humanitarian reasons." The American government saw this as a logical step in the execution of a policy of economic denial against the Castro regime, and one in line with the OAS resolution. Soon thereafter, on March 23, it also prohibited imports of merchandise made or derived in whole or part of products of Cuban origin. In conformity with the now established reactive hostility pattern, Castro responded to the OAS and American actions with a virulent speech—the famous *Second Declaration of Havana*.[29] In it, he not only called the Organization a "Yankee Ministry of Colonies," but also coined his most reverberating revolutionary phrase: "The duty of every revolutionary is to engage in revolution."

The world-shaking missile crisis, which centered attention on the Soviet-American confrontation in Cuba, was concluded in November 1962 with the Soviets withdrawing their missiles and long-range bombers from the island. Considering the generally accepted notions relative to the strategic missile balance between the U. S. and the Soviet Union at that time, the military value of the weapons systems in Cuba was viewed as highly threatening to the security interests of the United States. Their withdrawal, therefore, removed for the moment the fear of a direct strategic threat to the United States from Cuban territory.

Although Castro did not participate in the crucial negotiations between the leaders of the two superpowers—despite the involvement of Cuban territory in the controversy—he did subsequently refuse to allow any verification measures to be undertaken on Cuban soil. Thus, the Russians were unable to comply with their commitment to demonstrate that the weapons systems had, in fact, been effectively removed. Moreover, he opposed the acceptance of the American "no invasion" pledge in exchange for the establishment of inspection machinery, because, he said, the United States "has no right to invade Cuba and we cannot negotiate on the basis of a promise that a crime will not be committed."[30] A basis for negotiation could be arranged,

29. Martin Kenner and James Petras, eds., *Fidel Castro Speaks*, pp. 93-107 (Castro's speech of February 4, 1962).
30. Facts on File, *op. cit.*, p. 78.

24

he asserted, if the United States would agree to end (1) the economic blockade and all measures of commercial pressure, (2) all subversive activities, including the dropping and landing of arms by air and sea, the organizing of mercenary invasions, and the infiltration of spies and saboteurs, (3) U.S.-based pirate attacks against Cuba, (4) all violations of air and naval space by military aircraft and ships, and (5) the illegal occupation of Guantánamo and return the territory to Cuba.[31]

This phase is characterized by the activity that went into constructing the basic framework of the anti-Castro containment policy and the *intensity* of the American reaction to the supposed influence of "international communism" in Cuba—which reached somewhat exaggerated proportions. The following exemplifies the official U.S. policy line during this phase:

> As a bridgehead of Sino-Soviet imperialism within the inner defense of the Western Hemisphere, Cuba under the Castro regime represents a serious threat to the individual and collective security of the American republics and by extension to the security of nations anywhere in the world opposing the spread of that imperialism.[32]

The missile crisis had also sharpened tensions. And to make them even more acute, the American Congress saw fit to approve a joint resolution on October 3, 1962, which urged that steps be taken "to prevent by whatever means may be necessary including the use of arms, the Marxist-Leninist regime in Cuba from extending, by force or the threat of force, its aggressive activities..."[33] The missile crisis did represent, however, an important terminal point: it ended any American illusion that Castro could be eliminated through the mere application of pressure tactics. But the assumptions upon which the United States based its opposition to the Castro regime did not change. These are described quite aptly by Abraham F. Lowenthal:

> It was widely believed that Castro's Cuba represented the advance base of a Soviet (or even "Sino-Soviet") threat to U.S. interests in the area, and that the U.S.S.R. would seek other such bases. Cuba was thought to pose a potentially grave security threat to the U.S., directly because of its links with the international communist move-

31. *Revolución* (Havana), October 29, 1962.
32. *Department of State Bulletin*, January 22, 1962, pp. 129-130.
33. *Cuban Resolution*, Public Law 87-733 [SJ RES. 230], 76 STAT. 697, in *Legislation on Foreign Relations*, U.S. Congress, Senate Committee on Foreign Relations, House Committee on Foreign Affairs (Washington, D.C.: GPO, 1971), p. 743.

ment, and indirectly because of its support for subversive groups elsewhere in Latin America...It was expected that Castro's example would be followed elsewhere.[34]

Phase V. Refinement of the Containment Framework (1963-1968)

The general framework of the Eisenhower-Kennedy Cuban policy changed little during the years of the Johnson administration. The basic containment orientation did, however, become more elaborate and systematic through its multilateralization. Moreover, the exaggerated international communism threat-image perceived so strongly in the previous phase decreased only slightly.[35] Curiously, from time to time during 1963-1964 the Cubans publicly expressed a willingness to adjust mutual misunderstandings with the United States. They indicated, for example, that they would be willing to engage in a dialogue with the United States to discuss Guantánamo, trade "on the basis of mutual benefit," and even the possibility of providing indemnification for the nationalized properties.[36] But the United States chose to ignore them.

Nevertheless, still absent was a clear definition of the *ultimate* goal pursued by U. S. policy toward the Castro regime—a problem that even today is yet to be fully and satisfactorily resolved. The Johnson administration, following the example of its predecessors, continued to regard the Castro regime as *temporary* and envisioned the over-all goal of its policies to be the establishment of "a truly free and inde-

34. Abraham F. Lowenthal, "Alliance Rhetoric Versus Latin American Reality," *Foreign Affairs*, 48, 3 (April 1970), pp. 494-508.
35. In 1965, in the wake of the Dominican incidents, the House of Representatives resolved, related to the intervention of the international communist movement in the Western Hemisphere, that:
    "(1) any such subversive domination or threat of it violates the principles of the Monroe Doctrine, and of collective security as set forth in the acts and resolutions heretofore adopted by the American Republics;
    (2) in any such situation any one or more of the high contracting parties to the Inter-American Treaty of Reciprocal Assistance may, in the exercise of individual or collective self-defense, which go so far as to resort to armed force, and in accordance with the declarations and principles above stated, take steps to forestall or combat intervention, domination, control, or colonialization in whatever form, by subversive forces known as international communism and its agencies in the Western Hemisphere."
(*House Resolution 560*, September 20, 1965, in *Cuba and the Caribbean*, Hearings Before the Sub-Committee on Inter-American Affairs, Committee on Foreign Affairs, House of Representatives, Washington: GPO, 1970, pp. 33-34.)
36. Edwin Lieuwen, *The United States and the Challenge to Security in Latin America* (Columbus: Ohio State University Press, 1966), p. 33.

pendent Cuba which, under a government democratically chosen by the people, will live in peace with its neighbors." [37] Clearly, such a goal could be achieved only if the Castro regime were displaced by a Cuban government totally dedicated to liberal, democratic political principles—and not revolution.

The United States did come to the realization during this phase that the containment policy alone would not bring about the collapse of the Castro regime. Nevertheless, American policy makers were still confident that the people of Cuba would "not always be compelled to suffer under communist tyranny," and that only through freedom and democracy would they "be able to develop the high potential of their country for economic and social progress." [38] Thus, the United States not only refused to accept the Castro regime as legitimate, but also harbored the expectation that, in the long run, its over-all policy would be effective in creating the necessary conditions for the *eventual* overthrow of Castro. This, in turn, American officials believed would lead to the installation of a new government amenable to adopting a posture more in accord with the former traditional U. S.-Cuban relationship.

In an elaboration of the containment framework, the specific anti-Cuban measures already instituted by the United States were multi-lateralized through hemispheric approval and support. In July 1964, at the Ninth Meeting of Consultation of the Ministers of Foreign Affairs of the Organization of American States in Washington, the member states voted 15 to 4 to establish sanctions against Cuba on the basis of a complaint filed by Venezuela. In 1963, the Venezuelans had intercepted a three-ton shipment of arms destined for delivery to insurgent forces that were then actively engaged in a concerted effort to overthrow their constitutional government. A thorough OAS investigation revealed beyond doubt that the shipment had been a Cuban initiative. It was determined, therefore, that the Cuban arms shipment constituted aggression against Venezuela within the meaning of the Treaty of Reciprocal Assistance (Río Treaty). Accordingly, the following OAS sanctions were imposed against Cuba:

(1) the severing of diplomatic and commercial relations;
(2) the suspension of all trade, direct and indirect, except for foodstuffs, medicines, and medical equipment;

37. Robert M. Sayre, former Deputy Assistant Secretary of State for Inter-American Affairs, "Review of Movement of Cuban Refugees and Hemispheric Policy Toward Cuba," *Department of State Bulletin*, May 3, 1966, p. 712.

38. U. S. Department of State, *U. S. Policy Toward Cuba*, Department of State Publication 7690, Inter-American Series 88, 1964, p. 22.

(3) the suspension of all sea and air service to and from Cuba;

(4) the establishment of passport restrictions on travel to and from Cuba.[39]

At a similar conference in 1967 two additional actions were recommended as part of the sanction program against Cuba:

(5) the recommendation that government-owned or financed cargoes not be shipped on vessels sailing to Cuba;

(6) the general call to "Western" allies to restrict their trade and financial ties with Cuba.[40]

By 1964, then, the American containment policy toward Cuba—and its various supportive policy lines—had been considerably refined. The United States asserted categorically that there were two aspects of Cuban policy that it could not tolerate nor make the subject of negotiation: (1) Castro's support of subversion and insurgency in Latin America and (2) the regime's continued political, economic, and military dependency upon the Soviet Union. There was, then, no possible basis for a settlement of differences; Cuba could not acquiesce to the American demands without sacrificing its revolution. Therefore, in light of Castro's steadfast refusal to capitulate to American conditions—and the U. S.'s inability to force such a capitulation—the dual economic denial and political isolation policies had been strengthened as further support for the over-all containment policy framework.

Another major—and, in contrast, positive—step taken by the United States as a supportive measure within the containment framework was the *Alliance for Progress,* whose creation was clearly a response to the challenge and effects of the Cuban revolution. The official American rationale for the *Alliance* associates the purposes of the program with the threats of communism and subversion:

In the long run, however, Latin America will be rendered immune to communist infection only by an amelioration of the conditions —political, economic, and social—in which subversion flourishes. The United States and the free nations of Latin America have, therefore, through the Alliance for Progress, undertaken...the ambitious target of transforming the structure and productive capacity of

39. For background and texts, see *Department of State Bulletin,* August 10, 1964, p. 174.
40. *Department of State Bulletin,* October 16, 1967, p. 490.

28

the Latin American countries...But until such transformation is accomplished, Latin America will remain a fertile seedbed for communist subversion.[41]

The adopted supportive lines of action were directed toward several objectives. They were expected:

(1) to reduce the will and ability of the present Cuban regime to export subversion and violence to the other American states;

(2) to make plain to the people of Cuba and to the elements of the power structure of the regime that the present regime cannot serve their interests;

(3) to demonstrate to the peoples of the American republics that communism has no future in the Western Hemisphere;

(4) to increase the cost to the Soviet Union of maintaining a communist outpost in the Western Hemisphere.[42]

Although the Johnson administration viewed Castro and his revolution in Cuba in the same light as that of Eisenhower and Kennedy, the growing American involvement in Vietnam diverted its attention and energies from doing something more about the Castro nuisance. There is little doubt, however, that the administration's reliance on inherited attitudes and an over-estimation of the consequences of the potential threat of communist domination weighed heavily in the U.S. decision to intervene in the Dominican Republic in 1965, an action which represents a direct manifestation of American adherence to the "No Second Cuba" policy in the Caribbean.

Conclusion: Attitudes and Policy Change

U.S. policy toward the revolutionary regime in Cuba evolved on the basis of prevailing, hostile attitudes. U.S. policy makers under the Eisenhower, Kennedy, and Johnson administrations shared a common attitude—a dislike for Castro and for all that Fidelismo implied in Cuba, for Latin America, and vis-à-vis the United States. Presidents Kennedy and Johnson had arrived at the conclusion that the insolent Castro could not be tolerated, but, owing to the international power

41. U.S. Department of State, *U. S. Policy Toward Cuba*, pp. 10-11.
42. Former Under Secretary of State George Ball, "Principles of Our Policy Toward Cuba," *Department of State Bulletin*, May 11, 1964, p. 741.

configuration extending into Cuba through the Soviet Union, containment was the only viable alternative in the short run. Moreover, since at least 1963 it was thought that under the continued pressures, both external and internal, Castro simply would not last. For example, President Kennedy stated in 1963: "I don't accept the view that Mr. Castro is going to be in power in five years." [43]

Somehow, it was apparently believed, an unknown force would arise within Cuba to throw Castro out. This, in fact, became the principal assumption upon which U. S. policy was predicated. Once this occurred, the United States would then be prepared to accept *certain* modifications in Cuban society and in the country's relations with the United States. Nevertheless, it was further assumed that the hostilities of the past would be forgotten and a semblance of harmony and cooperation in the traditional pattern of U. S.-Cuban relations would be restored. Any other alternative was rejected as unsatisfactory.

The main point is, then, that through at least the end of the Johnson administration the United States refused adamantly to recognize that the Castro regime was firmly in control and not likely to disappear. This attitude was clearly manifested in this statement by Leonard C. Meeker, a high-ranking State Department official in the Legal Division:

...to settle the claims of U.S. nationals by the vesting and disposing of Cuban assets in this country implies no other means for settlement is foreseeable...That, in turn, could foster the impression that the United States accepts the Castro regime as a permanent feature of international life. *Nothing could be farther from U.S. policy.* [emphasis added] Our program is to apply continuing political and economic pressure on the Castro regime. That policy is manifested, for example, in the measures we have taken to restrict trade with Cuba, particularly measures related to shipping; in our travel regulations; and measures we have sponsored or supported in the inter-American system...All of these measures bear witness to our refusal to accept the Castro regime as a permanent fact of international life. [44]

Thus, American foreign policy makers developed a "moderate-intensity" [45] containment policy as the basic line of American strategy

43. Theodore C. Sorensen, *Kennedy* (N. Y.: Bantam Books, 1966), p. 814.
44. U. S. Congress, House of Representatives, *Claims of U. S. Nationals Against the Government of Cuba*, Hearings Before the Sub-Committee on Inter-American Affairs, Committee on Foreign Affairs (Washington, D. C.: GPO, 1964), p. 142.
45. See Chapter IX for an explanation of what is meant by a "moderate-intensity" containment policy strategy.

for dealing with Castro's Cuba. Hindsight shows that the strategy failed to have any appreciable effect on Castro's sources of internal support, but it did contribute to drawing the Cuban revolutionaries even closer to the Soviet Union. By this time Russia had committed its prestige and resources to the continuation of the socialist nation in the Caribbean. Castro proved to be less of a puppet than American policy makers had previously assumed, and Cuba was not exclusively serving Soviet purposes in the hemisphere, but the Cuban-Soviet relationship had become firm. The Soviets had to keep the regime afloat—and with little regard to cost.

This was the U. S. Cuban policy which the Nixon administration inherited in 1969. Just what changes and modifications have taken place since that date remain the topic of the following chapter, the sixth phase in the evolution of U. S. foreign policy toward the Castro regime.

CHAPTER III

U.S.-CUBAN
POLICY TODAY:
SUBTLE MODIFICATIONS

On an official level, the United States continues firmly wedded
to the rigid policy of opposition to the Castro regime. Official statements reaffirm that the basic conditions upon which the policy was
constructed subsequent to 1961-1962 have not changed in sufficient
degree to warrant essential modifications.[1] These conditions can be
reduced to the U. S. view of Cuba constituting a threat to the peace
and security of the hemisphere. Moreover, it is asserted that U. S.
policy is fully congruent with the decisions formally endorsed by the
Organization of American States. The threat is predicated on the basis

1. See Congressional testimony by administration spokesmen in: U. S. Con-
gress, House of Representatives, *Cuba and the Caribbean*, Hearings Before the
Sub-Committee on Inter-American Affairs, Committee on Foreign Affairs (Wash-
ington, D. C.: Government Printing Office, 1970); U. S. Congress, Senate, *Aircraft
Hijacking Convention*, Hearing Before the Committee on Foreign Relations
(Washington, D. C.: Government Printing Office, 1971); U. S. Congress, House of
Representatives, *Soviet Naval Activities*, Hearings Before the Sub-Committee on
Inter-American Affairs, Committee on Foreign Affairs (Washington, D. C.:
Government Printing Office, 1971); U. S. Congress, Senate, *United States Policy
Towards Cuba*, Hearing Before the Committee on Foreign Relations (Washington,
D. C.: Government Printing Office, 1971).

of (1) Castro's continued avowal—and in some cases active support —of attempts to subvert other governments in the region and (2) Cuba's military ties with an extracontinental power, i.e., the Soviet Union, whose presence there poses a danger for all the countries of the hemisphere.

To contain the Cuban threat, the United States operationalized a basically two-pronged offensive of political isolation and economic denial, along with aerial and naval surveillance of the island. Simultaneously, it sought to arrest the Castro contagion by strengthening the counter-insurgency capability of police and military forces throughout the hemisphere, while continuing to provide massive sums of economic and technical aid under the conceptual umbrella of the *Alliance for Progress*. Such tactics proved to be fairly effective in the past within the hemisphere. Nevertheless, they neither brought on the collapse of the Castro regime nor the effective cessation of unstabilizing forces and movements within the countries of the region. Today, the slowly widening gap in hemispheric solidarity limits their effectiveness even further. In the meantime, Cuba's military ties with the Soviet Union, if anything, have become closer. The general inertial tendency of the policy has served, then, to prolong an unnatural and mutually damaging adversary relationship.

Continuing Mutual Hostility

Despite moves by several Latin American nations to establish formal relations with Socialist Cuba, there has been no modification in the prevailing mutual hostility pattern between the two principal adversaries—the United States and Cuba. In fact, if anything, the official rhetoric coming from both sides has become more contentious. For example, Castro's line has not veered substantially from this bombastic assertion spoken on the eighteenth anniversary of the 26 of July in 1971:

> The Revolution will not retreat...we are not seeking conciliation of any kind with the Yankee imperialists...There will be no concessions of any kind to the imperialists.[2]

On the opposite side, the American position—to a degree more flexible but exuding a basic attitude of indifference—can be epitomized in these words by President Nixon:

2. *New York Times*, July 27, 1971, p. 10.

4

There will be no change, no change whatever in our policy toward Cuba unless and until—and I do not anticipate this will happen—Castro changes his policy toward Latin America and the United States.[3]

The obduracy inherent in the postures and attitudes of both countries, on the surface, has not diminished under the weight of speculation revolving around the implications of American and Chinese moves toward full rapprochement. But, despite Castro's apparent intransigence, it cannot be assumed that he flatly rejects the ultimate possibility of coming to some sort of accommodation with the United States. In fact, the tactic serves as an effective message to the United States. It puts the Americans on notice that accommodation is possible, but only if the United States is willing to deal with Cuba as an equal and is prepared to offer compensatory concessions.

It is important to bear in mind that Castro's concern for Cuban sovereignty has been the one wholly consistent theme in defining his government's international position. Even as early as mid-1959, Castro stated in reference to the possibility of coming to terms with the United States:

> We are ready to negotiate. They say that economic conditions can be discussed, but not communism. Well, where did they get the idea we would discuss that?...We have never even thought of the possibility of discussing our regime. We will discuss anything that will not affect our sovereignty. We are willing to talk. But does this mean we are aching to negotiate? Of course not. We are just taking a sensible step.[4]

The question becomes, then, the extent to which each country is moving toward a modification in the now long-standing hostility pattern. From the viewpoint of the United States, contrary to repeated public utterances, it is possible to demonstrate that the Nixon administration made what are in effect important yet subtle and still somewhat ambiguous changes in some basic aspects of its Cuban policy. Given time to mature, these may well provide the basis upon

3. *New York Times*, November 10, 1972, p. 20.
4. Castro television speech, May 21, 1959, taken from Martin Kenner and James Petras, eds., *Fidel Castro Speaks* (New York: Grove Press, Inc., 1969), pp. 76-90. A newspaper dispatch from Cuba, reporting an interview with two senior Cuban Foreign Ministry officials, quotes the latter as saying: "In any new relationship [with the U. S.] we demand respect for Cuba's independence and sovereignty; we demand this from all countries, including socialist countries." (*The Washington Post*, November 21, 1971, p. A22.)

which an eventual partial accommodation with the Castro regime can take place.

Key Policy Considerations

Direct military intervention to halt the Cuban revolutionary process ceased to be a feasible option from at least the time of the missile crisis in 1962. Instead, emphasis was placed on a policy of unmitigated hostility which, through economic and political isolation, sought four principal medium-range objectives: (1) to weaken the Castro regime (2) to discredit the Cuban economic model (3) to contain the spread of Castroism and (4) to weaken Cuba's ties with the Soviet Union by making support of the revolutionary regime so costly in political and economic terms that the Soviets would realize the futility of continuing its burdensome commitment there or of assuming similar commitments elsewhere in the hemisphere. If successfully attained, these objectives were to create the conditions for achieving the ultimate goal sought by the implementation of the "moderate-intensity" containment strategy: the eventual overturn of the Castro regime.

It is now recognized that the adopted policy, *in and of itself*, failed to achieve even the medium-range objectives. In the case of objectives (1) and (4), the policy proved to be counter-productive. On the one hand, the unrelenting U. S. opposition enhanced rather than diminished both the regime's will to survive and the support it garnered from the Cuban people by virtue of its ability to attribute many of the country's problems to the United States. On the other hand, the political isolation and economic denial actions, to the degree that they were successful, actually "pushed" Cuba into a closer relationship with the Soviet Union, since the latter was—and is—the only country besides the United States with sufficient resources to be able to subsidize the Cuban economy on a long-term basis.

There is no question that Cuba's economy was hurt by the economic denial program (objective 2), particularly because of its inability to acquire American replacement parts, machinery, and other essential goods necessary to keep its productive plant rolling. The fact is, however, that, despite the grave problems involved in completely reorganizing trade patterns and remaking its productive capacity, the economy did not collapse. Here, of course, major Soviet assistance was invaluable. Moreover, even Castro has candidly admitted that most of Cuba's economic problems have been due to internal and external factors only incidentally related to the effects of the econo-

35

mic denial program; the Cubans have made massive economic management and decisional errors which have compounded the difficulties inherent in transforming a basically capitalist economy into a highly centralized socialist system.

Finally, the spread of "Castroism," in the sense of revolutionary insurgency abroad, has not only been contained, but practically eliminated throughout the hemisphere (objective 3). But, its failure cannot be attributed solely to the actions instituted as part of the containment strategy. If "Che" Guevara's heroic Bolivian folly in 1967 proved anything, it was certainly that the "objective" conditions for revolution in Latin America are simply not yet present. Moreover, when and if revolution does come to any of these countries, outside forces will most likely play only a minor role. The policy did—and does—stand, however, as a clear reminder and warning to other groups and nations in Latin America of the limits to which the United States could exert its influence and resources should any of them be tempted to duplicate the Cuban example. The American public is today fairly resigned—owing to the unavailability of an effective means of removing it—to the continued presence of the Castro regime in Cuba. This is not to say, however, that U. S. policy makers are prepared to countenance any other nation in the region moving toward total alignment with a "hostile" state, or even the prospect of one coming under "communist" domination. The ghost of the Monroe Doctrine continues to stalk the American decision-making corridors.[5]

Now policy makers no longer claim that "a revolution in reverse is a revolution destroyed" or speak of depriving the revolution of "new successes *at home* or abroad." [6] Instead, the Nixon foreign policy team adopted a "low profile" for the region, stressing policy flexibility and a willingness to deal with governments "as they are" in the

5. The following congressional testimony illuminates the perpetuation of traditional U. S. attitudes toward Latin America:
"Mr. Gross: (Congressman from Iowa)
Let's get back to Cuba. We spent a lot of money in Cuba. We did just about everything for Cuba that we have for a lot of other Caribbean, Latin American, and South American countries. What happened? Where did the breakdown come in Cuba...What assurance do we have that, as with Cuba, it is not going to fall apart in our faces?"
"General Mather: (George R., U. S. Army, Commander-in-Chief,
                                     U. S. Southern Command)
The only way I can answer that, sir, is that we have not lost any more to date. There has been one Cuba. That was a rich learning experience."
(from U. S. Congress, *Cuba and the Caribbean*, p. 99.)
6. U. S. Department of State, Edwin M. Martin (former Assistant Secretary of State for Inter-American Affairs), *Cuba, Latin America, and Communism*, Department of State Publication 7621, November 1965, p. 3. Emphasis added.

36

hemisphere [7]—Cuba apart. But U. S. Cuban policy, they stated, was aimed only at the revolution's harmful "external" manifestations, and not at the substance and nature of the Castro regime or its particular brand of socialism. This is a highly significant distinction, which the administration began to make in 1971. Deputy Assistant Secretary Robert A. Hurwitch, the State Department's spokesman on Cuban policy, made this point several times. For example:

I wich to invite the committee's attention to the fact that...our concern is based upon external, not internal policies and activities of the Cuban government.[8]

Somewhat more than an exercise in semantics, this modification seems to represent a change in the objective of preventing Cuba from becoming a "model of communism." Such a judgment is made, however, with appropriate caution, for the United States likewise continues to assert that it seeks to reduce Cuba's capacity to export armed subversion and revolution. Obviously, an economically prostrate Cuba would not only lower this capacity, but also illustrate the ineffectiveness of the Cuban socialist model. In any event, the U. S. policy of political and economic isolation remains unaltered.

The Export of the Revolution

On the issue of Cuba's encouragement and support of violent revolution, no corresponding modification in U. S. attitudes has taken place. In fact, this issue has become the linchpin of current American policy toward Cuba—despite the U. S.'s professed desire to deal with the Cuban problem pragmatically. To maintain the elaborate anti-Cuban containment policy framework *merely* because of the complaint regarding Cuba's export of revolution would appear to be unreasonable, given the almost non-existence of Cuban-supported insurgency. Surely the solution to the U. S.-Cuban problem is not as simple as former Assistant Secretary of State for Inter-American Affairs, Charles A. Meyer, seemed to want to make it:

7. See the President's address before the Inter-American Press Association, Washington, D. C., October 31, 1969 (Department of State Publication 8501, Inter-American Series 97, Office of Media Services, Bureau of Public Affairs.)

8. U. S. Congress, Senate, *United States Policy Towards Cuba*, Hearing Before the Senate Foreign Relations Committee, (Washington, D. C.: Government Printing Office, 1971), p. 4. (See also U. S. Congress, Senate, *Aircraft Hijacking Convention*, Hearing Before the Senate Foreign Relations Committee (Washington, D. C.: GPO, 1971), pp. 76-77, and *The Washington Post*, April 13, 1972, p. A2.)

...I can see very little reason for us to seek to change our Cuban policy, particularly as Fidel clearly knows that all he has to do to wipe the slate clean is say, "I will no longer export revolution."[9]

Both Castro and the United States have by now seemingly left behind their particular policy illusions: the now sagging idealism of the *Alliance for Progress* and the resounding failure to export revolution via armed insurgency have taught both that revolution, as economic development or the implantation of democratic values, must and always will be fundamentally a national effort. Yet, the mutual hostility pattern developed between the two countries in the past apparently does not allow for an easy accommodation to new realities.

As a basic tenet of Cuba's revolutionary ideology and as a useful lever in Castro's relations with the socialist bloc, the *avowal* of revolutionary solidarity could hardly be dropped without perhaps irreparably weakening the onward progression and image of the Cuban revolution. But, as a matter of fact, Cuban instigation of revolutionary actions or direct Cuban infiltration into other countries to engage in subversive activities appear to be at present minimal and more costly to Cuba than dangerous to the various affected countries of the hemisphere.[10] Among the reasons given to explain the reduction of Cuban-instigated activities in the region are: (1) tough Soviet pressures (2) Castro's temporary acquiescence to the Soviet "peaceful" revolutionary strategy in Latin America and (3) Cuba's lack of material capability due to severely pressing economic conditions at home.

While any of the above explanations is plausible, one could credit Castro with being astute enough to recognize—particularly in view of Guevara's Bolivian fiasco in 1967—that the "objective" revolutionary conditions are simply not present in Latin America. He may well have judged, therefore, that it would be futile to become deeply engaged in expending energy and resources in marginal adventures which at this crucial juncture might seriously endanger Cuba's independent position in international politics—as well as the very preservation of its revolutionary experiment. Yet, State Department spokesmen publicly insist that, while Castro may be more "selective" in his attempts at subversion, the Cuban efforts in this respect continue unabated.[11] In reality, Castro's revolutionary activities in the hemisphere today pretty well boil down to providing training facilities

9. U. S. Congress, *Aircraft Hijacking Convention*, p. 69.
10. See U. S. Congress, *United States Policy Towards Cuba*, p. 6.
11. See, for example, the testimony of administration officials on Cuban policy in U. S. Congress, *Aircraft Hijacking Convention*, p. 88.

for small groups of hopeful insurgents and propaganda directed against most of the region's "non-revolutionary" governments.

Although public revelation of specific instances of Cuban subversion has not been made—purportedly "to protect intelligence sources" —The *New York Times* reported that in late 1970 American ambassadors were instructed to deliver the contents of a 25-page cable from the State Departament to the foreign ministers of all Latin American countries. The communication reportedly outlined specifics on Cuban activities and offered "citations from Premier Fidel Castro" to support the view that Cuba had yet to abandon its subversive purposes in the area.[12] There can be little doubt that Cuba maintains various centers for training in political subversion. But, as it has now been officially confirmed that only 2500 Latin Americans—mostly young leftist, non-communists—received training in Cuba during the period 1961-1969,[13] the implications of this aspect of Cuban activity call for thoughtful reassessment. During the 1960's, estimates generally reported numbers of "graduates" from these centers in excess of this figure for each year,[14] and no effort has ever been made to evaluate the intensity and effectiveness of this training. Moreover, surely it is a misreading of the dynamics of revolution to assume that so few even highly trained revolutionaries, by themselves and dispersed throughout a vast continent, are capable of inflaming or subverting the area. And, in fact, to any major extent this has not occurred.

Thus, a strong case could be made for encouraging the United States to underplay the Cuban potential for troublemaking in the hemisphere. Even administration spokesmen publicly recognize that Castro's ties with most of the area's guerrilla and urban terrorist movements are tenuous if not completely non-existent. Robert A. Hurwitch, former Deputy Assistant Secretary of State for Inter-American Affairs, has stated, for example:

12. *New York Times*, December 20, 1970, p. 23.
13. See U. S. Congress, *Soviet Naval Activities in Cuba*, Part 2, p. 16.
14. Former Secretary of Defense Robert McNamara is quoted in an interview for a national news magazine (*U. S. News & World Report*, February 10, 1964, p. 52) as stating: "Estimates of the number of Latin Americans being trained as guerrillas in Cuba run as high as 1500 at any given time." And, in 1967, a representative of the Defense Intelligence Agency (the same source which provided the figure cited in the text of 2500 Latin Americans trained in Cuba during the period 1961-1969) stated that "several thousand Latin Americans have been trained and indoctrinated in Cuba." (U. S. Congress, House of Representatives, *Communist Activities in Latin America*, Hearings Before the Sub-Committee on Inter-American Affairs [Washington, D. C.: GPO, 1967], p. 22.)

The other notable difference, I think is a shift from rural areas to urban areas. I think there is little question in my mind that some of the urban terrorism and some of the kidnapping that we have seen in the hemisphere is Cuban associated. I say associated in the sense that I would not wish to leave you with the impression that I think it is necessarily designed and controlled by Cuba. A number of people who have engaged in the terrorism in Guatemala and Brazil, to name two, are people who have spent some time in Cuba. It is, as I say, Cuban associated. It is not necessarily Cuban controlled or dominated.[15]

The ties that exist are fundamentally "inspirational." Deceased Brazilian guerrilla leader of the *National Liberation Action*, Carlos Marighella, stated in a published interview:

I am Brazilian. I am what revolutionary practice, carried out in the context of Brazil, has made of me. We follow our own path and if we emerge with views similar to those of Mao, Ho Chi Minh, Fidel, Guevara, etc., that's how things are...But, it you want to speak in terms of inspiration, we get ours mainly from Cuba and Vietnam.[16]

Besides, assisted by U. S. efforts to bolster their internal defense capabilities, the region's governments have proven to be capable of containing and even suppressing the small active subversive forces within their borders. Subversive groups, such as the *Tupamaros* in Uruguay, would exist with or without a Castro regime in Cuba. And, even if any of these countries were to re-establish diplomatic relations with Cuba, it seems reasonable to assume that they would be perfectly able to control Cuban interference through expulsions or, as an extreme measure, the unilateral and sovereign act of breaking off relations once again.

For U. S.-Cuban relations, the official recognition of the limits to Castro's effective export of revolution, coupled with the already announced acceptance of Cuba's internal political structures and social system, could well lead to a highly significant reduction in tensions between the two countries. U. S. policy makers simply have to refrain from emphasizing this aspect of Cuban activity. In the meantime, Castro revolutionary rhetoric should be discounted for what it basically is—pure rhetoric, differentiating clearly between the *proclamatory* and the *active* aspects of Cuban policy in the hemisphere. Then, should Cuban subversive activity remain low, or perhaps cease

15. U. S. Congress, *Cuba and the Caribbean*, pp. 26-27.
16. *Leviathan*, March, 1970, p. 36.

altogether, the United States could take quiet credit for offering a cue which encouraged the other side to take the initiative in removing one of the principal blocks which today effectively assures the continuation of the mutual hostility syndrome. The problem, of course, would be that, without the rationalization of Cuban subversion, U. S. policy makers would be left with little upon which the present course of their Cuban policy could be justified. As noted before, Cuba's *support* for the export of revolution has become the fundamental *official* U. S. complaint and the rationale for the maintenance of the oppositionalist policy strategy.

The Cuban-Soviet Military Relationship and U. S. Policy

Much more complex and difficult to perceive are indications of policy modifications which revolve around the threat of Cuban military ties with the Soviet Union. It is here where, particularly, the lines of long-range strategic considerations and U. S.-U. S. S. R. relationship join with the Cuban-U. S. policy pattern. Moreover, the question has become still further complicated in the wake of the controversy generated over Soviet naval intentions in the Caribbean and the meaning of the purported American-Soviet "understanding" concerning sea-based, offensive weapons systems.[17]

With direct Soviet assistance, Cuba today has probably the best equipped armed forces of any Latin American country. Moreover, on a *per capita* basis, it has by far the largest. The London-based *Institute of Strategic Studies* estimates that the Cuban armed forces consist of 109, 500 men with 185 combat planes.[18] There is, in addition, an armed militia force of approximately 100,000. In spite of this the United States has never considered that this force constitutes a danger either to its territory or to that of neighboring Latin American countries, since Cuba lacks the necessary air and sealift capacity to mount offensive operations outside the island. What has concerned the United States, however, are reports of "excessive" amounts of arms being supplied to Cuba. The worry here is that Cuba could export the excess for direct support to hemispheric subversive movements.

17. The implications of this development are discussed within a case study framework in Chapter VI.
18. *New York Times*, September 4, 1970, p. 6. Most U. S. officials give a much higher estimate, generally in the neighborhood of 200-250,000 men in Cuba's standing, organized armed forces. The confusion probably centers around the exact role and numbers of the Cuban militia. Brazil, with eleven times Cuba's population of 8.8 million, has a military establishment of only 194,350 men.

Although the transshipments of arms by Cuba is presently severely hampered by U.S. sea and air surveillance of the island, U.S. concern will probably persist so long as Russia is prepared to supply the Cubans with large quantities of arms—and the United States, in turn, considers such arms a danger to hemispheric security. In fact, however, an administration spokesman has admitted that "there is no evidence that the U.S.S.R. has furnished arms or training to Cuba for the specific purpose of supporting violent revolution in Latin America." [19] This American concern thus seems to serve as merely a pretext for the continuation of the anti-Castro containment policy.

On the other hand, a still very obscure aspect of the Cuban threat continues to be the meaning assigned to the policy objective of limiting or eliminating altogether Cuba's military ties with the Soviet Union. During the 1960's, the United States objected not only to the Soviet-supplied arms, but also even to the very presence of the Russian military on the island. [20] In this respect, the United States has indeed made a turnabout which represents a distinct policy modification. While never made explicit in official policy statements, officials have indicated in congressional testimony that the United States would not dispute Cuba's "right" to have military assistance programs, complete with Soviet military advisers and equipment, provided that such equipment and training would be for defensive purposes only. [21] An appropriate clarification of this point may well be in order as a helpful device in tension reduction.

Conclusion: Exploratory Conciliation

U.S. Cuban policy today has moved from the basically static containment framework elaborately developed during the Kennedy-Johnson years of the 1960's to a status quo but semi-conciliatory posture toward the Castro regime. The change is not only significant, but remarkable, if one recalls that the inclination toward accommodation was carried forward by an administration headed by a man who, in 1964, said:

19. U.S. Congress, *Soviet Naval Activities in Cuba*, Part 2, p. 7.
20. Assistant Secretary of State for Inter-American Affairs Edwin M. Martin said in 1963:
"...we shall spare no effort to induce the Soviet Union to continue to remove its military personnel from the island...we will not relax our pressure until all these forces are gone from the Caribbean."
(from Martin, *Cuba, Latin America, and Communism*, p. 2.)
21. U.S. Congress, *Aircraft Hijacking Convention*, p. 77, and confirmed in an interview with a ranking State Department area official, September 1971.

42

Rather than a policy of flexibility, of softening, of conciliation, we must have a strong and determined policy...[this nations's troubles stem] from not standing firm against communist dictators—it is time to end this disgraceful and self-defeating behavior.[22]

Thus, on the one hand, the same attitudes of disdain for Castro's arrogance and intransigence persist in sustaining the basic hostility pattern directed against Cuba's "maximum leader"[23] and the revolutionary government, while formally maintaining the supportive action lines embodied in the established containment policy. On the other hand, however, the slight yet highly meaningful and suggestive alteration in fundamental aspects of the policy has inclined the general policy orientation toward a tempering of hostility and a more realistic appraisal of primary national interests.

In line with its over-all hemispheric policy, the United States has made a deliberate attempt to concentrate on only those foreign policy factors in the region that affect American "vital" interests directly. Few interests can be considered intrinsically vital. But certainly in the case of Cuba, ever since the missile crisis of 1962, the only concern even remotely approximating such a classification would be the implications of the Soviet fleet visits and the possible use of Cuban territory in enhancing the capacity of a strategic, offensive weapons system directed against the United States. And even this, with time, will become less significant. When the Soviet missile-bearing, atomic submarines become available for deployment in the Caribbean in large numbers, the usefulness of Cuban territory will lessen correspondingly.

Other American interests somewhat inferior to the "vital" category are, nonetheless, obviously part of the Cuban equation. These include a concern for future political developments within Cuba and the long-range implications of Cuba's place in the future configuration of politics in the Caribbean. A growing American concern for shaping

22. Richard Nixon, "Cuba, Castro, and John F. Kennedy," *Readers Digest* (November 1964), p. 300.

23. An extreme example of personal contempt for Castro affecting rational judgment is the following comment made by Dante B. Fascell, Congressman from Florida and Chairman of the House Sub-Committee on Inter-American Affairs:

"I might add a personal note. I made a speech some years back that was rather critical of the Castro government. He responded in his political newspaper that Fascell was an international gangster, part of a conspiracy to overthrow his government. I would like to get that retracted some time before we start to talk to the guy."

(from U. S. Congress, *Cuba and the Caribbean*, p. 22.)

a desirable political and economic environment for the area in the future depends on policy actions taken today. And Cuba must figure predominantly in such calculations. While less obvious than in the case of China, for the Caribbean, geography and economic facts compel that the Cuban presence be taken into account. A prolongation of the over-all containment policy has become untenable, for it fosters the very aspects which the United States considers most objectionable: internally, it enhances the increasing sovietization of Cuban society while, externally, the American obsession with Castro facilitates the Soviet penetration of Latin America [24] and assures the continued Soviet use of Cuba for its naval purposes.

Fundamentally, the United States has now taken a big first step toward dealing realistically with its Cuban problem, even though, in essence it is merely an indication of a willingness to listen to a Castro plea for change. As such, it is not only an inactive initiative, but also condescending and certain to fail in eliciting a favorable response from Castro. Not surprisingly, Castro's anti-American harangues have continued unabated, while the Nixon administration went so far as to renew the unenforceable passport restrictions on American citizens for travel to Cuba. Whatever benefits there might be in moving toward some type of political accommodation are as deeply concealed now as before. In the face of other priority items, the United States apparently finds its present Cuban posture satisfactory and accepts Cuba's increasingly tightened dependence upon the Soviet Union. Thus, despite realistic modifications in some elements of its Cuban policy, the U. S. is not yet prepared to seek actively the settlement with Cuba—similar to the one with China—which must eventually take place.

24. See Chapter V for discussion on this point.

PART II

THE OTHER PRINCIPAL ACTORS AND THEIR OUTLOOKS

CHAPTER IV

THE CUBAN REVOLUTIONARY REGIME: ITS FOREIGN POLICY GOALS AND PERSPECTIVES

Be it an interpretation of the past, an estimate of the future, or even a view of the present, judgments made on or about the Cuban revolutionary regime are simply not subject to test. Lack of access to pertinent data, materials, and key decision makers makes empirical verification, at present, impossible.[1] Yet, only through the construction of some notion regarding the nature of the regime, its decision-making structures and policy goals, as well as its relationship to communism and the communist party-state system can one arrive at some estimate of the latitude and limits of Cuban behavior in determining future policy options open to the United States. Judgments can be made on certain aspects of the Cuban political environ-

1. American scholars, on occasion, have been permitted to visit Cuba. Once there, however, access to valid information regarding the questions raised here would still constitute a perhaps unsurmountable problem. Informed estimates remain, therefore, as the only basis for rendering opinions about most attitudes, values, processes, and structures of today's Cuban society—to say nothing about aspects which determine its foreign policy behavior. This writer found himself doubly disadvantaged: not only was a trip to Cuba impossible, but also, despite repeated communications, even the Cuban mission to the United Nations in New York refused to agree to a discussion of these questions in a personal interview.

ment which have a bearing on American foreign policy considerations; but, for the most part, they will not be a product of verifiable research. The following discussion, although somewhat speculative, represents a distillation of viewpoints and conclusions found in available literature, as well as more personal evaluative judgments.

Cuban Foreign Policy: Decision-Making and Paramount Policy Objectives

Central to an understanding of the Cuban political process is the role of Fidel Castro. In the United States, foreign policy decision-making is part of a political process involving conflict and consensus among a multitude of constituencies. It is, moreover, essentially a product of a vast and complex bureaucracy which purposively *attemps* to seek information, set goals, and analyze the implications and consequences of alternative behaviors by relating the varying expected outcomes to the established objectives. The impact, therefore, of individual personalities *may* be decisive, but more often this factor represents merely one in an assemblage of variables whose presence can have a decided bearing on policy outcomes.

For Cuba, in contrast, not only foreign policy but all public policy carries the engraved personal impression of Castro and the loyal coterie that surrounds him. Moreover, through a continuity in key power roles, this revolutionary leadership continues as the exclusive spokesmen for the regime and the party. Even some sympathetic observers have lamented the continuing "cult of personality" as the hallmark of the revolutionary regime. In their view, this has constituted an effective obstacle to the institutionalization of the revolution. American Marxists Leo Huberman and Paul M. Sweezy note, for example:

> In practice, however, the relation between government and people continued to be a paternalistic one, with Fidel Castro increasingly playing the crucial role of interpreting the people's needs and wants, translating them into government policy, and continuously explaining what had to be done, and what obstacles remained to be overcome.[2]

And, even though it is relatively unrestrained by veto groups within Cuban society, the revolutionary leadership has not been required to

2. Huberman and Sweezy, *Socialism in Cuba* (New York: Monthly Review Press, 1969), p. 204. For a similar view, see also Edward González, "Castro: The Limits of Charisma," *Problems of Communism* (July/August, 1970), pp. 12-24.

48

excessive coercion in garnering support for its policy objectives and positions.[3]

Thus, at the heart of the regime remains the charismatic appeal of Fidel Castro. This appeal cements public support for policy decisions which are a product of an unsystematic but highly pragmatic intercourse between the elements that make up the leadership group. Thus far the *modus operandi* of the regime has precluded the existence of even relatively open political forums. However, for the vast majority of Cubans still on the island, the regime and its policies are viewed as legitimate; those who oppose Castro and his goals have, for the most part, already departed. Furthermore, indications are that those who continue to leave do so not so much for ideological reasons, but for a personal inability to cope with demands placed on the general citizenry as the regime attempts to come to grips with its ambitious developmental objectives, or for sentimental reasons and the desire to be reunited with relatives or friends outside of Cuba.[4]

Given the impediments inherent in attempting to carry out a thoroughgoing socialist revolution in an underdeveloped country whose economy and political structure had previously been closely bound to a close and powerful neighbor, it is hardly surprising that Castro's policies, both internal and external, have vacillated radically. Nonetheless, in terms of the goals toward which Cuban policy has been directed, they show considerable consistency. Above all, the Cuban revolution has been and is fundamentally nationalistic—a desire to make the country, to the extent possible, sovereign, autonomous, and independent. To accomplish this, Castro's principal goal has remained constant: the survival of the revolution. Thus, Cuban policy

3. In view of the total absence of public opinion surveys in Cuba, it is at present impossible to gauge the depth and extent of public support for the revolutionary regime and its policies. The existing surveys conducted during the early years of the revolution showed overwhelming support for Castro and his government—about 87 % of the general populace in favor of the regime, with even higher percentages recorded among the young and the rural elements. (See Raúl Gutiérrez Serrano, "El pueblo opina sobre el gobierno revolucionario," in *Bohemia*, No. 26, June 26, 1960, pp. 49-50; Lloyd A. Free, *Attitudes of the Cuban People Toward the Castro Regime*, Princeton, N. J.: Institute for International Social Research, 1960.) Based on data gathered during 1962, another study showed that support for the regime, while still high, had declined somewhat. The results showed 70 percent favorable. (See Maurice Zeitlin, *Revolutionary Politics and the Cuban Working Class*, Princeton, N. J.: Princeton University Press, 1967.)

4. The most systematic and extensive study on exile motives and beliefs is Richard Fagen, Richard A. Brody, and Thomas J. O'Leary, *Cubans in Exile: Disaffection and Revolution* (Palo Alto, California: Stanford University Press, 1968).

5

has been directed toward (1) attaining security against American opposition and (2) maintaining support for the regime and its goals through vigorous and uncompromising developmental efforts designed to bring economic and social betterment to the Cuban people. In so doing, Castro has proved to be highly pragmatic, rather than a rigid ideologue. An example of this has been his oscillating views on the "correct" method of revolutionary struggle in the hemisphere.

During the mid-1960's, the Castro line was that revolutionary victory could be achieved only through violence—or the so-called *vía armada* revolutionary strategy. At other times, Castro has espoused a view more closely in harmony with the Soviet *vía pacífica* strategy, which opposes sole reliance on armed struggle, urging, instead, that the communist parties and other "revolutionaries" seek small niches of power within the respective political systems of Latin America.[5] Castro has since qualified Cuba's former hard-line position on insurrection. This latest change, which took place in 1968-1969, was underlined by Cuban communist Carlos Rafael Rodríguez:

> Cuba believes that armed struggle is the fundamental instrument for the advancement of the revolutionary process in the majority of the Latin American countries, and will continue to support this thesis. This concept has often been misinterpreted in the belief that it means that armed struggle is indispensable in each and every country of Latin America.[6]

Today, Cuba endorses all forms of opposition in the struggle for revolution in the hemisphere. This demonstrates, then, the degree to which Castro has not allowed ideology to interfere with the pursuit of Cuba's nationalistic principles. Regis Debray provided this pertinent description of Castro's pragmatism:

> A Leninist is an opportunist with principles. Fidel is a Leninist. His principles remain firm, but the oportunities change. The unique thing about him is the combination of great realism in the evaluation of the means available and the final goal.[7]

Castro's adherence to the nationalistic principle of securing Cuban independence has, however, in some ways worked against the counterpart developmental goals of the regime. In the beginning, Cuba

5. See W. Raymond Duncan, "Soviet Policy in Latin America Since Khrushchev," *Orbis*, Vol. XV, No. 2 (Summer 1971), pp. 642-669.
6. *Granma* (Havana), June 15, 1969.
7. *La Opinión* (Buenos Aires), August 28, 1971, p. 13.

may well have derived greater direct advantages by establishing an international position of unalignment in the hope of obtaining benefits from the two contending superpowers. But American opposition to the regime's revolutionary goals prompted Castro to seek international support for what he perceived as the U. S. threat toward the revolution. To survive, Cuba could not afford to become isolated; it needed both protection and economic assistance to underwrite its ambitious developmental plans. Thus, in an adroit linking of foreign policy to domestic goals, Castro actively sought Russian support while proclaiming the desirability and need for armed revolution, Cuban-style, throughout Latin America. By pursuing these policies, he hoped to preclude the possibility that through isolation his revolution would fall.

Cuba's Relationship to Communism, the Soviet Union and the Communist Party-State System

The Cuban Communist Party, the PSP,[8] took no part in Castro's revolutionary efforts until Batista's overthrow late in 1958 became clearly evident. The party had, in fact, previously denounced Castro's 1953 attack on the Moncada Barracks as a "bourgeois putschist adventure." By mutual agreement, however, PSP members did participate in anti-Batista actions in exchange for Castro's assurances that the party would subsequently not be persecuted. And later, with the progressive radicalization of the revolution, Castro increasingly turned to the Cuban communists for internal support and as allies in encouraging the Soviet Union to accept the unorthodox Cuban communist regime into the socialist camp,[9] thereby assuring the regime of a Soviet commitment to its survival in political, economic, and

8. The official communist party organization changed its name during World War II—when it was participating in the government—from the *Revolutionary Communist Union* (URC) to the more innocuous *Popular Socialist Party* (PSP). With the advent of the revolution, it became absorbed and submerged within the Castro-dominated revolutionary movement. Thus, in July 1961, the PSP became linked to Castro's *26-of-July Movement* and the *Student Directorate* (DE) through the organizational instrumentality known as the *Integrated Revolutionary Organizations* (ORI). This, in turn, became the *United Party of the Socialist Revolution* (PURS) in February 1963. Finally, in October 1966, although its membership remained unchanged, the official revolutionary organization became know as the *Cuban Communist Party*. It is still totally dominated by Castro.
9. Edward González persuasively develops the argument that Castro used the Cuban communists by soliciting their aid in convincing the reluctant Soviets to take on a dubious Cuban commitment. That the Soviets did respond—despite the

military terms. Both the old-line communists and the official party itself have, however, played ancillary roles in the development of the revolutionary process.[10] Despite instances of internal infighting, Castro remains today the dominant power and fully in command. Castro communism is still *sui generis*, hardly congruent with other existing varieties; it is, in short, what Castro says it is.

Castro's turn to the Soviet Union brought mixed blessings to both countries. For Cuba, economic realities turned Castro's independence ambitions into a practical dependency upon the Soviet Union; Russia and other socialist countries swiftly replaced the United States as Cuba's principal trading partners.[11] A material dependence has not meant, however, an ideological dependence. Although now firmly committed to Cuban support,[12] the Soviets have found Castro to be

---

ideological and security risks inherent in such a commitment—González attributes to Castro's perceptive exploitation of cold war and communist intra-systemic politics. This reasoning prompts him to conclude, then, that Castro's switch to a militant, anti-American stance was founded on the need to (1) justify his overtures to Moscow (2) affirm Cuba's independence and (3) provide an external enemy, thereby facilitating his efforts to charge the internal political climate with a dedicated, combative atmosphere. (See González, "Castro's Revolution, Cuban Communist Appeals, and the Soviet Response," *World Politics*, Vol. XXI, No. 1 (October, 1968), pp. 39-68.)

10. The key leadership positions in the party continue to be dominated today by Castro and his 26-of-July stalwarts, with the party structure headed by Castro himself. The old-line communists have been relegated to vastly inferior power positions (except for Carlos Rafael Rodríguez). Moreover, the role of the party itself remains as yet amorphous; personalistic decision-making persists as the continuing norm in the Cuban political system.

11. The rapid changeover in Cuba's international trade patterns is here graphically and strikingly presented:

Distribution of Foreign Trade
(percentages)

Exports to Cuba

	1958	1962
Socialist Countries	2.6	86.7
United States	66.8	1.0
Others	30.6	12.3

Imports from Cuba

Socialist Countries	.03	80.3
United States	69.8	0.0
Others	29.9	19.7

(From Stephen Clissold, ed., *Soviet Relations with Latin America: 1918-1968*, Oxford University Press, 1970, p. 266.)

12. The Soviet leadership has many times reaffirmed the solid basis of the

a troublesome maverick, and the history of the two countries' relationship has not been entirely smooth. Even though the Soviets considered that their interests were furthered by being in Cuba, they became engaged there by accident rather than design. And they have found their commitment to be not only economically costly, but also potentially dangerous in light of the nationalism of the sometimes quixotic Castro. The Cuban leader has shown himself to be hardly amenable to every Soviet guideline and policy objective. Concluding a Castro visit to the Soviet Union in 1964, for example, the official communique contained a reference to Cuban independence which, by inference, was obviously directed toward the Soviets:

> But the Cuban Government would not permit anyone to intervene in the internal affairs of its country. The path of development of its state—the path of socialism—chosen by the Cuban people, is the Cuban people's own, inalienable, affair.[13]

Internally, Castro has so far been able to keep the Soviets at an arm's length, both directly and by not allowing the pro-Soviet, old-line communists to assume too much power within the party hierarchy or through key government power positions. In 1962 Castro struck out against communist Aníbal Escalante—and other elements of the old PSP—for alleged "sectarian" activities. And once again, in 1968, he singled out Escalante for leading a "microfraction" within the revolutionary leadership group for carrying out:

> ...attacks, by means of intrigues, on the principal measures of the revolution; the distribution of clandestine propaganda against the line of the party; and attempt to proffer distorted orientation to several nuclei of the party; the presenting of false, calumnious data about the plans of the revolution to officials of foreign countries with the intent to undermining [sic] the international relations of Cuba with other governments; the taking of secret documents from the Central Committee and the furthering of ideological diver-

---

U.S.S.R.-Cuban ties. Soviet party leader Brezhnev stated at the 24th Party Congress in 1971:
"Over the years the Central Committee has devoted constant attention to strengthening cooperation with the Republic of Cuba and the Communist Party of Cuba. As a result of joint efforts, considerable successes have been achieved in developing Soviet-Cuban relations. The peoples of the Soviet Union and of Cuba are comrades-in-arms in a common struggle, and their friendship is firm." (In *New York Times*, March 31, 1971, p. 14.)
13. *Cuba Socialista* (Havana), February 1964.

gences among certain militants who came from the ranks of the People's Socialist Party.[14]

Whether these attacks by the Cuban leader were meant to be a deliberate and direct warning to the Soviets not to interfere in Cuban internal affairs is still a debatable question. They had the effect, nevertheless, of reaffirming Castro's position in the revolutionary process, and of strengthening Cuban independence vis-à-vis the Soviet Union by not allowing the more servile, pro-Soviet communists to gain an upper hand.

Such incidents, plus open disagreement on other issues, have strained, but never completely disrupted the Cuban-Soviet relationship. Over the years the contending issues have encompassed: (1) the effective power role of the Cuban Communist Party (the Russians would prefer it to be more in line with Eastern European practices) (2) Cuba's ideologically-heretical notion that communism and socialism can and should be developed simultaneously (3) Cuban displeasure with the Soviet Union's backdown in the wake of the missile crisis (4) differing views on the correct revolutionary strategy for Latin America (5) a divergence of opinion over the pace and emphasis of Cuba's economic development (6) Cuba's insistence on *moral* over *material* incentives and (7) Cuba's neutrality in the Sino-Soviet rift, to list only a few. Yet, despite the disputes, the Cuban-Soviet "alliance" remains unaltered.

Since at least 1968, such ongoing Soviet-Cuban controversies as remain have become muted as Castro has increasingly turned his attention to pursuing pressing domestic economic concerns in the development area—particularly the herculean efforts made in 1970 to achieve the promised 10 million ton sugar harvest.[15] Since then, Cuban economic performance has continued to lag, and the Soviet Union has been persistent in insisting upon assurances that its massive aid and assistance be effectively employed for the ends and results commonly agreed upon by both parties. In trade terms alone, the Soviet Union's imbalance of exports to Cuba clearly indicates the extent to which the former must increasingly carry the burden for Cuban development through indirect subsidy.[16] Indeed, American of-

14. Quoted from Leo Huberman and Paul M. Sweezy, *Socialism in Cuba*, p. 210.
15. The 1970 sugar crop totaled 8.526 millions tons, somewhat short of the desired level, but still the highest ever obtained in Cuban history.
16.

Trade of the Soviet Union with Cuba, 1966-1970
(Value in thousands of United States dollars)

ficials estimate that, over-all, the Cuban debt to the Soviets is now well in excess of $ 3 billion.[17]

Castro's amplified interest in domestic concerns has corresponded with a diminution of attention to hemispheric revolution, even in official rhetoric. This seems to be more than a fugacious episode or a deliberate tactical ploy: since at least 1968, Cuban instigation of subversion has been notably curtailed. Whether this dwindling enthusiasm for continental revolution proves transitory or permanent, it indicates for the moment a convergency with Soviet strategy in the hemisphere. Moreover, domestically, Castro agreed to the establishment, in December 1970, of a *Soviet-Cuban Intergovernmental Economic, Scientific, and Technological Cooperation Commission*[18] expressly designed to assure the most effective employment of Soviet assistance. The end result is, however, an even deeper Soviet involvement in the furtherance of Cuban internal developmental programs through the penetration of Cuba's increasingly more formalized decision-making structures. For the *Intergovernmental Commission* is charged with the responsability of formulating Cuba's over-all economic planning; and this is crucial in an economy as highly centralized as that of revolutionary Cuba. Additionally, as of 1972, Cuba has become a member of *COMECON*, the Soviet bloc's economic union.

Thus, although the extent to which Cuba's policies are today dictated by the Soviet Union cannot be conclusively established, should the trend toward an increased reliance on Russia continue, Castro could well end up falling into the very trap he has so far successfully

Exports		
U. S. S. R. to Cuba	1966	479,000
	1967	563,000
	1968	624,000
	1969	624,000
	1970	700,000
Imports		
U. S. S. R. from Cuba	1966	285,900
	1967	327,800
	1968	277,800
	1969	231,700
(year of record sugar crop)	1970	535,000

(From *Value Series, Communist Areas-Trade, 1966-69,* International Trade Analysis Division, Bureau of International Commerce, United States Department of Commerce, May, 1971, and the same series for 1970, published in September, 1971.)

17. See U. S. Congress, House of Representatives, Committee on Foreign Affairs, *Soviet Naval Activities in Cuba,* Part 2, Washington: GPO, 1971, p. 12.

18. Headed by, significantly, Carlos Rafael Rodríguez, the one important

eluded—that of almost total dependence upon the Soviet Union and the loss of the cherished Cuban independence.

Conclusion: Cuban Foreign Policy Goals Today

But if the experiences of the Cuban revolution prove anything at all, it is certainly that Castro's uncanny ability to dominate the mutations that have developed in the unfolding of the revolution should not be underestimated. This ability may, in fact, provide a partial explanation of Castro's apparent decision to play down the promotion of armed struggle in other hemispheric countries. And it might also give a clue to his more relaxed attitude toward newly-emergent "revolutionary" regimes in Latin America, like the military-populist government presently in power in Peru [19]—and, of course, the former Marxist government in Chile. He may well have in mind, in other words, the possibility of obtaining maximum economic support from the Soviet Union during this crucial development period while simultaneously working to increase his political maneuverability. The latter he could achieve, first, by coming to terms with a number of Latin American governments outside the formal organizational framework of the inter-American system and, later, with the United States.

Castro knows that a partial settlement with the United States would not mean total Soviet withdrawal. For political and ideological reasons alone, Russia would never consent to the loss of a communist ally or ever conspire with an "imperialist-capitalist" country, i.e., the United States, against Cuba. This would not preclude the possibility, however, that both Russia and the United States might not be agreeable to establishing parallel positions, with Cuba as the beneficiary of partial support from both sides. [20] But even in this hypothetical case,

---

old-guard Cuban communist who has managed to survive within the shifting revolutionary power structure.

19. The Cuban newspaper *Granma* (May 3, 1970, pp. 2-5) carried an article which contained this pertinent official government statement:

...[Cuban] support does not necessarily have to be expressed in favor of guerrilla movements, but [can be extended to] any government which sincerely adopts a policy of economic and social development and of liberating its country from the Yankee imperialist yoke. No matter by what path that government has reached power, Cuba will support it."

(quoted in González, *Problems of Communism*, p. 22.)

20. This point is made, in a different context, by W. Averell Harriman in *America and Russia in a Changing World* (Garden City, N. Y.: Doubleday & Co., Inc., 1971), p. 204.

in all probability the Russians would continue to underwrite Cuban socialism with economic and military assistance; the United States would merely agree to establish mutually-advantageous political and commercial ties with Cuba. In any event, the significance of this scenario for Cuba and Castro would reside in its propitious prospects for preserving Castro's fundamental foreign policy objectives—independence, survival of the revolution, and maintenance of the Castro regime.

Developments over the past few years indicate, then, that the overall Cuban national goal of survival of the revolution has come to mean, for Castro, the elimination of underdevelopment at home instead of violent revolution in the hemisphere. Castro has stated publicly:

> We are no longer engaged in an ideological battle as we were at first. Now it is a battle in the economic field.[21]

Castro will doubtless continue to give lip-service to Cuba's support of revolutionary struggle—which over the years has been exaggerated by Castro, the United States, and the governments of Latin America—thereby stressing inspirational influence and example rather than expansion of the present minimal material efforts. In the meantime, he will seek to widen Cuba's commercial relationships with Western countries and forge new diplomatic links in the Western Hemisphere [22] while attempting to maintain an independent role within the communist party-state system.[23]

21. Quoted in *Visión* (Mexico), June 3, 1972, p. 68.
22. Mexico, Canada, and Jamaica in the Western Hemisphere maintained diplomatic or consular ties with Cuba without a break. During 1972, actual diplomatic exchanges with Chile and Peru presaged the decisions of Guyana, Barbados, Argentina, Panama, and Trinidad-Tobago, and Venezuela to establish official relations with Socialist Cuba—all despite the still operative anti-Cuban sanctions of the Organization of American States.
23. The condition of Cuba's independent position within the communist party-state system is developed in full by Daniel Tretiak in "Soviet and Chinese Policies Toward Cuba and Cuba's Response," Paper read at the 69th Annual Meeting, American Political Science Association, September, 1970, copyright, American Political Science Association, 1970, and additionally in "Cuban Relations with the Communist System: The Politics of a Communist Independent, 1967-1970," ASG Monograph No. 4, Waltham, Mass.: Westinghouse Electric Corp., Advanced Studies Group. Another important study which concentrates on Cuba's ideological struggles within the hemisphere is D. Bruce Jackson, *Castro, the Kremlin, and Communism in Latin America* (Baltimore: The Johns Hopkins Press, 1969.)

CHAPTER V

COMPLETING THE TRIANGLE:
THE CORE INTERESTS OF
THE SOVIET UNION IN CUBA

Cuba's uneasy status as a revolutionary communist independent within the increasingly heterogeneous international party system has placed many demands upon its principal mentor, protector, trading partner, and purveyor of economic and military assistance—the Soviet Union. Above all, Cuba's increasingly close relationship with the Soviet Union has created for the latter a basically ideological core interest which commits it to sustaining Cuba's fundamental goals of survival and national development. Nonetheless, the Russian entrenchment in Cuba has served Soviet strategic and tactical interests, particularly in relation to its objectives in the Western Hemisphere and to its long-range goals vis-à-vis the United States.

The Cuban-Soviet Relationship and Soviet
Objectives in Latin America

In the beginning, the Soviet Union was pleased with the victory of the Cuban revolutionary forces, and even more so when the new regime evidenced, through its actions and words, a determination not to yield to the United States in the prosecution of its internal and

58

external goals. Conflict between the United States and Cuba was inevitable. It was an unequal contest to be sure, but one which was bound to further the long-range goal of the Soviet Union in Latin America—the acceleration of the volatile nationalistic, anti-American impulses present in the region. In short, the conflict would help to undermine the U. S. power position and influence in the area long regarded as America's "backyard." At first, anything even approximating a full and permanent commitment to the Castro regime was far from being contemplated. After all, the new regime's capacity to survive was still very much in doubt. And certainly the island's remoteness and vulnerability were additional factors that made the Soviets hesitate before committing their prestige and resources in support of Castro and his revolutionary goals. But developments in the hostile U. S.-Cuban context, particularly the abortive Bay of Pigs invasion, encouraged them to be even more responsive to Castro's willingness to accept Russian assistance.[1]

Castro needed the Soviet Union as a shield against expected U. S. aggression and as a major source of essential economic and developmental assistance.[2] He also needed its market for Cuban sugar. All this he obtained not only as the result of cold war politics, but also through his skillful exploitation of ideological rifts within the communist world itself. By 1963, Cuba was officially accepted into the communist party-state system. Consequently, the Soviet commitment

---

1. Soviet economic support for Cuba dates from February 13, 1960, or before the regime's break with the United States. At that time the Soviets agreed to buy one million tons of Cuban sugar and to extend the regime a $ 100 million credit. Furthermore, the Soviets agreed to pay for 20 % of the sugar in freely convertible currency and the remaining 80 % in Soviet goods at international prices. Even before this agreement, however, the Soviet Union had been buying fairly sizeable quantities of Cuban sugar—for example, $ 15 million in 1957. This was paid in U. S. dollars and no corresponding Soviet exports were involved. (See The Cuban Economic Research Project, *A Study on Cuba*, Coral Gables: University of Miami Press, 1965.)

2. The People's Republic of China, which established diplomatic relations with the Castro regime in September 1960, signed a trade agreement with Cuba in October of the same year. The Chinese agreed to buy one million tons of sugar during 1961 and to extend a credit of $ 60 million. The touchy Cuban-Chinese relationship reached a low point in February 1966 when Castro attacked them for "interfering" in Cuban internal affairs and for reneging on their pledge to buy that year's 800,000 ton quota of Cuban sugar, as well as to supply the full amount of the promised 250,000 tons of rice. Although relations between the two countries have cooled considerably in light of Castro's seeming attachment to the Soviet line in the ongoing Communist ideological dispute, trade has continued on a reduced scale, totaling approximately $ 70 million in each direction in 1970. (See "Fidel Castro," in *Peking Review* (February 25, 1966), pp. 16-20, and *Granma* (Havana), February 6, 1966.)

to Cuba has come to mean that it cannot allow Cuba to fall militarily, to collapse internally, or to fail economically.

Soviet acceptance of Cuba into the socialist camp—and the concomitant obligations this decision created—was not taken, however, without some calculation of benefits in terms of strategic advantages for the Soviet Union. In the first place, although Latin America has a low priority as a region in the over-all Russian strategic view for the advancement of Soviet and communist objectives in the world,[3] the continuing existence of a revolutionary, socialist regime in Cuba was considered important. Cuba has added considerable symbolic value to Russia's encouragement of anti-U. S., nationalistic fervor. This, in turn, has accentuated the subtle but recognizable trend throughout the area toward an "independent" foreign policy posture—away from submission to the United States. One aspect of contemporary Latin American nationalism seems to be a close association between socio-economic change internally and "independence" in foreign affairs. Thus, with Cuba as the embodiment of this nationalistic spirit, the Soviet objective of urging these countries to counteract or even repudiate U. S. influence was effectively being fulfilled.

Secondly, besides Cuba's usefulness as a model for socialism in the hemisphere, the U. S. S. R. was not blind to its strategic potential for the furtherance of Soviet economic, political, and military objectives in the area. To a point, this potential has been exaggerated by the United States. For, in fact, Castro's control of Cuban politics has placed a definite constraint on Soviet desires to pursue its broader strategic ends by using Cuba directly or through attempts to impose limits on Cuban behavior. Moreover, the Soviet commitment to Cuba definitely adds an additional degree of uncertainty to Soviet global calculations in terms of its maneuverability vis-à-vis the United States. Nevertheless, it is only necessary to recall the missile crisis of 1962 to provide an excellent example of a Soviet attempt to draw on Cuba as a strategic resource. Today, a decade later, with technological advances in modern weapons systems coupled to modifications in international power relationships, even the reintroduction of land-based missiles in Cuba would change only slightly any general, over-all global advantage for the Soviet Union in the spiraling contest between the superpowers for ultimate military security. Dr. Henry A. Kissinger, National Security Adviser to the President and now Secretary of State, has provided a telling analysis of the contemporary international

3. Herbert S. Dinerstein, "Soviet Policy in Latin America," in David S. Smith, ed., *Prospects for Latin America* (New York: Columbia University, The International Fellows Program Policy Series, 1970), pp. 135-145.

system. Some of his comments have a bearing on this point:

> The international situation has been undergoing a profound structural change since at least the mid-1960's...Each of us [the U.S. and the U.S.S.R.] has just [sic] come into possession of power single-handedly capable of exterminating the human race...With modern weapons, a potentially decisive advantage requires a change of such magnitude that the mere effort to obtain it can produce disaster... In other words, marginal additions of power cannot be decisive.[4]

But Cuba does provide the Soviets with a geographic location in the Caribbean from which, in a sense, they can counter the American forward base strategy. This does not require the actual existence of Soviet bases in Cuba. In fact, any overt move to install military bases there having a strategic potential would doubtless trigger a heavy U. S. response. But under the doctrine of freedom of the seas, the Soviet Union has, since 1969, made small-scale, intermittent, and gradual deployments of elements of its fleet into the Caribbean—and without official protest from the United States. Given, then, the Soviet Union's determination to expand its world-wide naval activities,[5] the pretext of making friendly business visits to Cuba has most certainly facilitated its move into the Caribbean. In any real sense, even a sustained Soviet naval presence in this area will not change the over-all strategic balance; it does, nonetheless, complicate American defense efforts and provides the Soviets with a tool with which to counter the hitherto absolute American supremacy in the area.

A third area of potential use of Cuba by the Soviet Union is the much discussed communist strategy for the subversion of Latin America. It is on this point that the Soviet Union and Cuba have, at least in theory, found themselves at odds in recent years: Cuba was aspiring to leadership in the Latin American struggle by extolling violence (the *vía armada*) as the only road to revolution in the area;[6] the

4. *The Washington Post*, June 16, 1972, p. A18.
5. U. S. Chief of Naval Operations, Admiral Thomas A. Moorer, stated: "The Soviet's ocean operations are becoming unmistakingly more aggressive, more varied, and being conducted in ever-increasing distance from their home bases."
(from "Growing Threats of Soviet Sea Power," in *U. S. News & World Report*, January 20, 1969, p. 49.)
6. For those who wish to explore the ideological boundaries of the Cuban revolutionary spirit, Regis Debray's *Revolution in the Revolution?* (New York: Monthly Review Press, 1967), is a must. In this work, the young French intellectual carefully outlines the Cuban revolution's distinguishing characteristics, its strategy, and its lessons: that in Latin America an insurrectional *foco* can create

Soviet Union, in diametrical opposition, was urging peaceful evolution and a gradualist view (the *vía pacífica*) toward the eventual emergence of socialism in the region. There is little question that this ideological dispute has proved somewhat disruptive to relations among anti-establishment, revolutionary groups in Latin America. And, in some cases, it has been conducive to a splintering of the orthodox communist parties. Moreover, at times it has strained, without ever coming near breaking, the ever-closer relationship between Moscow and Havana. But as a consequence of this now largely non-existent controversy over the preferred and more correct tactical method for achieving revolutionary success in the region, a highly distorted notion has become widely propagated: the Soviet Union is seen as fully committed to peaceful evolution toward socialism; Castro's image, in contrast, is blown all out of proportion as a wild-eyed, dangerous, and impetuous radical revolutionary.

From a tactical standpoint, the Soviets indeed do counsel their adherents in Latin America to work for the development of anti-imperialist fronts and participation in electoral politics; meanwhile, on their own, the Russians are making considerable efforts to build and reinforce diplomatic and trade relationships with governments of all political complexions in Latin America.[7] Thus, in opposition to prevailing current assumptions, the Soviet Union may actually gain more from the existence of the highly vocalized, revolutionary belligerency emanating from Cuba than if Castro decided to fall completely in line —rhetoric and all—with the Soviet's Latin American policy posture.[8] Moscow's search for respectability and the position of the Soviet-backed communist parties in the region are, therefore, decidedly

---

revolutionary conditions; that popular forces can win in a prolonged struggle against the institutional armed forces; and that, fundamentally, the countryside must be the locale for the Latin American revolutionary struggle. Debray's views on the "correct" method of revolutionary struggle have since changed; he now accepts a plurality of forms, except for countries like Argentina and Brazil, where he sees armed-struggle as the "key" path. (See the Debray interview in *La Opinión* (Buenos Aires), August 28, 1971, pp. 11-14.)

7. The Soviet Union now has formal diplomatic relations with 12 Latin American countries. Its trade with the area (except for Cuba) remains, however, fairly static, representing only about 2-4 % of the region's total world trade—and most of this with Brazil and Argentina (see U.S. Congress, House of Representatives, *Cuba and the Caribbean*, Hearings Before the Sub-Committee on Inter-American Affairs, Washington: Government Printing Office, 1970, p. 36.)

8. This reasoning follows closely that of Peter Schenkel, "Cuba's Relations with the Communist World," in J. Gregory Oswald and Anthony J. Strover, eds., *The Soviet Union and Latin America* (New York: Praeger, 1970), pp. 146-158. Mr. Schenkel served on Castro's economic planning commission (1960-1966) and was Cuba's Minister of Industry during 1964-1966.

enhanced so long as the stigma of revolutionary inspiration and the fury of repression can continue to be placed on Cuba's doorstep. As a consequence, then, Soviet policy can turn a two-fold profit: its image as a subversive agent will be reduced in Latin America while, by virtue of its sustained assistance to Cuba, the Soviets can continue to project their professed ideological image as an ally of the Third World in the struggle against imperialism and underdevelopment.

The conventional view, in short, sees the split between Moscow and Havana on revolutionary strategy as highly detrimental to the interests of the communist movement in Latin America. The conclusion reached in this analysis is, however, the exact reverse—at least from the standpoint of a long-range perspective. In reality, it would actually work to the disadvantage of the Soviets should Castro give up even his present half-hearted efforts in support of armed insurrection, most of which consists of pure oratory. The truth is that neither Cuba nor the Soviet Union gives much support to active insurgent groups in the region. In fact, some of these groups openly repudiate both Moscow and Havana in preference to their own nationalistic strategies and goals. Pertinent here are some comments made by former Brazilian revolutionary leader Carlos Marighella. When asked if his guerrilla group received arms and money from Cuba, he answered: "No. There are more arms and money here in Brazil than in Cuba. One of the imperatives of our struggle is to take arms and money from the enemy. This weakens it and creates an atmosphere of revolutionary war." And when questioned about the significance of peaceful coexistence, he quipped: "That is a Soviet problem. For us, people of the Third World, that is not even viable." [9] Moreover, the possibility of revolutionary success by any of today's radical movements is practically nil. There is little chance, therefore, that these insurrectional activities could compromise the Soviet Union by compelling it to assume major support burdens, and thereby place it in direct confrontation with the United States. At the same time, Cuba does not need to follow the Soviet course of moderation simply to assure continuing Russian aid. For the reasons noted, the Soviet Union has little choice but to give assistance. The reason for the reduction of Castro-inspired violence seems to be simply his realization that, in the absence of the necessary "objective" conditions, the promotion of armed struggle is not now profitable. It does mean, however, that Castro is now compelled to seek other ways of asserting Cuba's independence in the face of its growing dependency on the Soviet Union.

9. *Leviathan*, March, 1970, p. 37.

Conclusion: Strategic Status Quo in the Hemisphere

Despite the disruptive influence of Castroism and the efforts of the Soviet Union to make strategic inroads in the region through Cuba, the essence of the international balance has not been altered. The United States remains today the paramount power in the Western Hemisphere. Nevertheless, it is toward the Soviet Union and not Cuba that the major thrust of U. S. preoccupation and concern should be directed—even though this, too, can be exaggerated.[10] The Latin American governments that seemingly have been eager to establish diplomatic and trade relations with the Soviet Union have done so for the very practical reason of hoping thereby to reduce somewhat their considerable economic dependency on the United States while expanding the market for their products. Moreover, this fits in well with their nationalistic desire to have a more independent foreign policy. There is no intention on their part, however, to cut themselves off completely from the United States and turn to the Soviet Union. Even the Marxist government of Salvador Allende in Chile attempted to avoid this very distasteful and harmful alternative. The correct view of Soviet policy in the hemisphere is, therefore, very aptly stated by one American scholar:

> The Soviet Union views Latin America as lying within the sphere of influence of the United States. At the maximum, therefore, the Soviets would like to see governments which are independent enough from State Department policy so they will establish diplomatic and commercial ties with Russia and perhaps offer some resistance to United States military intervention. At the same time Soviet policy makers hope these independent governments do not become too identified with the Soviet Union, thereby imposing heavy economic and political obligations on the U.S.S.R.'s economy and government. The Soviets are not interested in becoming involved in another Cuban-type situation.[11]

10. Referring to the issue of the renewal of diplomatic relations between Colombia and the Soviet Union in January 1968, a congressional report stated: "In one bold stroke the Soviets acquired a new, strategically located operational base in the Caribbean region and an opportunity to advance locally its long-term strategy of communist world revolution." (from U. S. Congress, House of Representatives, Sub-Committee on Inter-American Affairs, Committee on Foreign Affairs, *The New Strategy of Communism in the Caribbean,* by Armistead F. Selden, Jr., Washington: Government Printing Office, November, 1968, p. 14.)

11. James Petras, "The United States and the New Equilibrium in Latin America," *Public Policy,* 18:1 (Fall, 1969), p. 108.

Paradoxically, the U.S.'s over-all hemispheric posture coincides closely with that of the Soviet Union: both represent a species of "low profile" projection, exemplified by a willingness to deal with governments of the region "as they are." For the United States this purportedly means a less assertive role in Latin American affairs and a readiness to engage in new partnership relationships while, for the Soviet Union, it seems to indicate a long-range, gradualist Soviet strategy in the hemisphere. The general inertial tendency of these policy orientations tends to remove Castro's Cuba from the center of U.S.-U.S.S.R. concerns. And, perhaps it is only Castro who can upset this new equilibrium.

CHAPTER VI

A RUSSIAN SUBMARINE BASE IN CUBA?: STRATEGIC CONSIDERATIONS AND THE IMPLICATIONS OF THE AMERICAN-SOVIET "UNDERSTANDINGS"

Directly related to U. S. Cuban policy is the issue highlighted in the famous missile crisis of 1962—the willingness of Cuba to lend its territory to the Soviet Union for strategic purposes. The issue then was presumably settled on the basis of the agreement concluded between President Kennedy and Chairman Khrushchev through exchanges of letters and public pronouncements, most of which have been made public.

In the aftermath of the crisis, the Soviet Union seemingly concurred in Kennedy's assessment, outlined in his speech of November 20, 1962, that "... if all offensive weapons are removed from Cuba and kept out of the hemisphere, under adequate verification and safeguards, and if Cuba is not used for the export of aggressive communist purposes, there will be peace in the Caribbean."[1] It should be recalled that the United States, for its part, agreed to lift the quaran-

1. The text of this speech and all pertinent documents are included in the document section of Robert F. Kennedy's *Thirteen Days: A Memoir of the Cuban Missile Crisis* (New York: Signet Books [The New American Library, Inc.], 1969), pp. 131-186.

tine measures then in effect and to give assurances against an invasion of Cuba. This was contingent, however, upon (1) Russian removal of its offensive weapons systems from Cuba and (2) Soviet concurrence in establishing arrangements to assure that such systems would not be reintroduced.

Castro, who was totally eclipsed during the crucial Kennedy-Khrushchev negotiations, later stymied the on-site inspection arrangements by the International Red Cross or the United Nations. Effective verification for the removal of the missiles did take place, nevertheless, when Russia agreed to close-in overhead and naval inspection of their returning ships by U. S. air and seacraft. But, in the absence of permanent safeguards, the United States insisted upon continuing U-2 surveillance flights over the island without harrassment. This was considered essential as a precaution against similar future emplacement of Soviet offensive weaponry. These reconnaissance overflights have continued intermittently since that period without incident, even after 1964 when the Soviet SAM's (surface-to-air missiles) were placed under Cuban control.

Since Kennedy tied the no-invasion pledge "to appropriate U. N. observation and supervision," it is often argued that the United States became unbound from its part of the commitment. In fact, however, by the end of 1962 the United States declared itself satisfied that the Soviet Union had withdrawn all its offensive missiles and bombers from Cuba. Thereby, in effect, the United States accepted the surveillance overflights as a substitute for on-site inspection. On April 20, 1964, a State Department representative referred to the continuation of these flight by stating, in part:

I would recall that the overflights are a substitute for the on-site inspection agreed to by the Soviets in October, 1962, but which Fidel Castro refused to permit...I would remind you of the various statements made by the late President Kennedy and by Secretary Rusk during the past fifteen months on this subject, making it unmistakably clear that we regard the overflights as a necessity to avoid the deception which was practiced against us in 1962.[2]

Thus, although there is no explicit statement by the U. S. government regarding a reinterpretation of its no-invasion pledge, the meaning is clear that no such action would take place so long as the surveillance flights continue unmolested.

Following the missile crisis, U. S.-Cuban relations settled into a low-keyed belligerency as more pressing international problems com-

2. *Department of State Bulletin*, Vol. 50, May 11, 1964, p. 744.

peted for the time and energies of the United States government and public. Freed from the immediate danger of the Soviet strategic threat in Cuba, the United States seemed content to rely on the dual policies of political isolation and economic denial as long-term measures for dealing with the nuisance of its Cuban problem. Even at this time, the possibility of an eventual Soviet naval thrust into the Caribbean area was being discussed. It was still too early, however, to expect that this development might require a corollary "understanding" amending the agreement reached after the missile crisis. In fact, the Soviets gradually increased the frequency of their naval squadron visits to Cuba, particularly in 1970. Even so, administration spokesmen reported no evidence of Soviet naval base construction activities in Cuba, although the possibility was not discounted "as long as Castro's hostility to the United States persists." [3]

In the meantime, unconfirmed reports of Soviet construction in the vicinity of Cienfuegos Harbor abounded throughout 1970. The administration at first desisted from making provocative accusations or from even commenting on the possibility of a Soviet base there. Then, on September 25, 1970, a *New York Times* article by C. L. Sulzberger underlined the possibility of a new Soviet base in Cuba to service Russian *Yankee*-class, missile-carrying, nuclear submarines. That very day—perhaps too coincidentally—both the Department of Defense and the White House [4] called press conferences at which carefully prepared statements alluded to this matter.

Jerry W. Friedheim (Deputy Assistant Secretary of Defense for Public Affairs), for example, implied that U-2 intelligence [5] indicated unusual Soviet construction at Cienfuegos and that the presence of a 9,000 ton *Ugra*-class tender and barges there were among "the indications that make us feel that the Russians want to establish a base." [6] Henry Kissinger, speaking for the White House, reminded the Soviets of Khrushchev's 1962 promise to keep "all weapons systems capable of offensive use" out of Cuba and the hemisphere. He then proceeded to state quite explicitly: "The Soviet Union can be under no doubt that we would view the establishment of a strategic base in the Caribbean with utmost seriousness." [7]

3. U. S. Congress, House of Representatives, Committee on Foreign Affairs, *Cuba and the Caribbean*, Hearings Before the Sub-Committee on Inter-American Affairs, Washington: Government Printing Office, 1970, p. 103.

4. Identified as Presidential Assistant Henry Kissinger in a subsequent *New York Times* article of January 5, 1971, p. 1.

5. Confirmed in personal interviews with State Department area specialists, September 1971.

6. *New York Times*, November 15, 1970, p. 1.

7. *New York Times*, September 26, 1970, p. 1.

Quite possibly, the administration was forewarned of the Sulzberger article and believed it necessary, in order to avoid a possible disruptive public or congressional outcry, to downplay a crisis atmosphere through selective yet firm public statements. This was seemingly important from the domestic political standpoint of the pending congressional elections. Moreover, it may well have been deemed as required in view of the delicate tension-reducing posture adopted by the administration in its relations with the Soviet Union.

The public revelation of a possible naval base in Cuba, and not the actual presence of Soviet ships there, apparently caused the administration to issue its warning. For, only a few days earlier in a backgrounder given on September 16, a White House spokesman had declared "that the simple presence of these ships is not in itself inconsistent with the letter of the 1962 American-Soviet agreement on keeping Russian nuclear weapons out of the hemisphere." [8]

No immediate comment on the U. S. warning was forthcoming from the Soviet Union, nor was it reported that the United States attempted to press the issue through direct diplomatic communications with Moscow. The public reaction in the United States was, over-all, mild. Senator J. William Fulbright cautioned that to assume the Soviet Union had no right to establish such a base in Cuba was at best "a questionable proposition." [9] Congressman Mendel Rivers, nevertheless, warned of a "new Soviet threat at our very doorstep" and urged the administration to "take every diplomatic, and if necessary, military step" to eliminate such a base.[10]

Shortly thereafter a House sub-committee queried intelligence agency spokesmen on the situation. The latter described the construction on Alcatraz Island in Cienfuegos Harbor as "two possible barracks-type buildings, a few other buildings, repair of a pier, and construction of a probable soccer field and other recreation facilities." [11] They termed the facility at Cienfuegos as one "which might support naval operations in the Caribbean area, including submarines," but were careful to distinguish this from the connotations of a base: "It is by no means to be construed, I think, as a formal full-scale base. It is a support facility, a possible support facility." [12]

8. *New York Times*, October 4, 1970, Section IV, p. 3.
9. *New York Times*, September 26, 1970, p. 1.
10. *New York Times*, September 28, 1970, p. 17.
11. U. S. Congress, House of Representatives, Committee on Foreign Affairs, *Soviet Naval Activities in Cuba*, Hearings Before the Sub-Committee on Inter-American Affairs, Washington: Government Printing Office, 1971, p. 16.
12. *Ibid.*, p. 7.

It is important to keep in mind here that the U.S. government officially acknowledges that Soviet missile-bearing, nuclear submarines already operate off the eastern coast of the United States. Thus, by providing protective shelter for essential repairs and rest and recreation facilities for the crews, a Cuban base would merely augment the Russian offensive striking power to the extent of increasing its ability to maintain the limited number of *Yankee*-class, nuclear submarines now available for commitment to this general maritime area. Defense Secretary Melvin Laird, on the other hand, estimated that a Cuban base would increase the "threat potential" of this weapons system by 33-40 %.[13] His calculation was based on the view that a Cuban base would reduce the number of long trips to and from the submarines' home base in Murmansk, estimated to be 12-17 days for each round-trip.

While Secretary Laird's assertions may well be true, it seems an exaggeration for him to claim that this new Soviet facility, if operational, would in itself "shift the strategic balance." If anything, it would represent a small tactical advantage for the Soviet Union. And it seems highly unlikely that the Soviets would have wanted to risk jeopardizing the areas of broader vital importance with the United States—or risk a new confrontation—for this small gain. Besides, it is still unclear whether, indeed, the Soviets even wanted to establish a full-scale nuclear naval base at Cienfuegos. The presence of the tender, as well as the periodic visits by Soviet fleet vessels, doubtless represent Russia's resolve to assert a right to expand naval operations to any or all international waters. But, because of American sensitivities regarding this traditional U.S.-dominated area, the move into the Caribbean had to be accomplished carefully.

At no time did administration officials claim that even the Soviet tender had in fact serviced nuclear submarines at Cienfuegos or in Cuban waters. Secretary Laird did say, however, that he "assumed" Russian sailors had used the facility there for recreation.[14] There is no evidence to doubt this statement, and Soviet naval use of Cuba will assuredly continue. However, the principal point is that, with increasing numbers of Soviet missile-bearing submarines becoming operational, the use of Cuba as a naval base may be convenient but hardly necessary as a means of heightening the strategic threat to the United States from the Caribbean.

Finally, on October 9, 1970, political observer V. Matveyev in an *Izvestia* article ruled the U.S. concern over a naval base in Cuba as

13. *New York Times*, December 3, 1970, p. 2.
14. *New York Times*, October 13, 1970, p. 5.

"groundless," and stated that the Soviet Union intended to adhere fully to the 1962 U. S.-U. S. S. R. agreement. He also observed that Cuba concurred in this position.[15] This was followed by an official Soviet denial of the American allegations through a statement distributed by *Tass*. In it, the Soviet Government accused the United States of "fanning the war psychosis." The supposed violations were viewed as a "concoction," and it stressed that Russia was doing nothing to "contradict" the 1962 agreement. The statement also emphasized that it was universally recognized that any sovereign state, including Cuba, could allow Soviet ships and vessels to enter its ports for "official visits and business calls."[16] At that time the United States accepted the Soviet statements as adequate responses to its warning of September 25. State Department press officer Robert McCloskey said the following day: "They say they are not; we say that we regard that as a positive statement and I have no information to the contrary."[17]

Although the American press insisted that the McCloskey response was conditioned by seven weeks of prior diplomatic consultation with the Soviet Union, no concrete evidence exists that such consultation did take place. In the meantime the Soviet tender at Cienfuegos left port on October 10, but returned again on November 10, the latter even after the "secret" meeting in New York City on October 22 between Dr. Kissinger, Soviet Foreign Minister Andrei A. Gromyko and Soviet Ambassador Anatoly F. Dobrynin. It was widely conjectured that during this meeting private assurances were given regarding the expanded meaning of the 1962 American-Soviet agreement.

There can be little doubt that the United States and the Soviet Union have come to some tacit understanding regarding the possible utilization of the naval facility at Cienfuegos. To conclude from this, however, that precise conditions or stipulations have been similarly agreed upon must be regarded as an assumption that does not emerge from available evidence. Otherwise, the confusing subsequent declarations of various American spokesmen on the exact meaning of the agreement would not have occurred. For example, on December 2, 1970, Secretary Laird agreed that the accord would not preclude the servicing of nuclear submarines "outside of Cuban waters."[18] Later, however, President Nixon in an interview asserted that the servicing of nuclear submarines "either in Cuba or from Cuba" would be "a violation of the understanding." And that, despite his further

15. *Izvestia*, October 9, 1970.
16. *Tass*, October 13, 1970. Transcript.
17. *New York Times*, November 14, 1970, p. 4.
18. *New York Times*, December 3, 1970, p. 2.

71

comment to the effect that the understanding had been "so clearly laid out... and clearly relied on by us." [19]

To confuse matters still further, on the day following the President's statement, the White House once again "clarified" its definition of what constituted a violation of the new understanding. This time, officials stated that the servicing of nuclear submarines by tenders based in Cuba was prohibited "anywhere at sea" [20] instead of only in the immediate area of the Caribbean. They also indicated that the Soviet acceptance of the "understanding" had been affirmed on October 13, 1970, the date of the official *Tass* statement.

From the foregoing, it can only be concluded that no real understanding was reached between the United States and the Soviet Union regarding the limits to which Cuba might be used for Soviet naval purposes in the Caribbean. For the present, the very vagueness of the tacit accord serves the mutual purposes of both sides, but could be challenged by either at any time. Basically, its "provisions" consist of unilateral declarations by the United States. Therefore it is not so certain, in the words of one unidentified foreign affairs official, that "we believe we have an understanding with the Soviet Union in which both sides know the limits beyond which the situation would become grave." [21]

Indeed, there is still the uncertainty over whether the Soviet Union wanted—or even needed—to turn Cienfuegos into a naval base on the order of the American installations at Holy Loch, Scotland and Rota, Spain. But, it seems quite certain that the United States would hardly launch an invasion of Cuba to remove a small-scale naval supply and recreation facility. Moreover, we have Castro's unusual reticence on this issue, which could well be explained by the fact that it was never intended to become an obvious target for American retaliation. And undoubtedly Cuba will continue to be used by the Soviets for certain naval purposes.

The real importance of Cuba today for the Soviet Union—besides its symbolic value as an outpost of socialism in the hemisphere—is that by the very existence of a friendly, pro-Soviet state in this strategic area, the Soviet Union has established a precedent for moving into the region. This has allowed the Soviet Union to claim a "right" to expand its fleet activities into a sensitive new maritime area considered highly vital to the security of the United States. The Soviet naval presence in the Caribbean is now a *fait accompli*.

19. *New York Times*, January 5, 1971, p. 21.
20. *New York Times*, January 6, 1971, p. 14.
21. *New York Times*, February 14, 1971, p. 2.

PART III

U.S. CUBAN POLICY: THE CONTROLLING VARIABLES AND POLICY ALTERNATIVES

PART III

U.S. CUBAN POLICY
THE CONTROLLING
VARIABLES
AND POLICY
ALTERNATIVES

CHAPTER  VII

POLICY PATTERNS, DOMESTIC CONSTRAINTS, AND AN EXAMINATION OF POLICY OBJECTIVES

Mutual rancor and recrimination continue to underlie the persisting discordant U. S.-Cuban relationship. As indicated in preceding chapters, this self-perpetuating hostile orientation, based now on largely fixed threat-images, has produced a foreign policy context in which doctrinaire rigidity tends to replace a more rational framework for effective policy formulation. Moreover, the situation is further intensified by the complicating implications surrounding the presence and role of the Soviet Union in Cuba.

In terms of American diplomatic history, the resulting pattern of mutual hostility characterizing U. S.-Cuban relations since the advent of the Cuban revolutionary regime is not entirely unique. A similar fundamentally antagonistic and reactive policy was adopted by the United States in two earlier instances involving communist states—the Soviet Union from 1917 to 1933 [1] and the People's Republic of

1. Certain aspects of the Soviet case are surprisingly congruent with the fundamental attitudes and irritants in the U. S.-Cuban dispute. According to Averell Harriman, even as late as 1926, many people were still predicting that

China from 1949 to 1972. In both cases, the United States reacted to the communists' revolutionary successes by pursuing a policy grounded on enmity, non-recognition, and isolation. This is not to say that the onus for the adoption of such a policy rests entirely on the United States. The syndrome is characterized by a competitive animosity that encourages *both* sides to ignore how their own actions and strident rhetoric sustain and even reinforce the mutually threatening images. And certainly in this case the United States and Cuba can both point to enough concrete instances of grievances and outright provocations to make the antagonism seem genuine.

The basic focus of this inquiry has been the degree to which there has been movement toward a modification in the intransigent hostility pattern. And by the way of summary and clarification, the findings relevant to this point can be reduced to the following conclusions and judgments:

For the United States

1. The intransigent nature of the U. S.'s anti-Castro posture fails to square with its present over-all foreign policy orientation which seeks to avert acute tensions and to come to sensible accomodation with communist governments.

2. In the Western Hemisphere the United States professes a desire to reduce overt U. S. involvement in Latin America's internal affairs and to deal with governments "as they are."

3. The emergence of a freely-elected Marxist government in Chile and other "progressive" regimes in Latin America, e. g., Peru, which the U. S. views as legitimate, has to an important degree conditioned U. S. attitudes to accept a coexistence with radical regimes in the hemisphere.

4. With the passage of time the intensity of American moralizing involvement in Cuban developments has diminished.

5. Various components of the over-all anti-Cuban containment policy design have become increasingly tenuous and difficult to justify in light of changing circumstances, e. g., the continued emphasis

---

the communist regime in Russia would not last five more years; and, as in the case of Cuba, the U. S. government's principal complaints against the Russians were (1) the financial claims of U. S. nationals and (2) communist subversive activities, the latter referring to Moscow's "support" and money for subversion within the United States. (See W. Averell Harriman, *America and Russia in a Changing World* [Garden City, N. Y.: Doubleday & Co., Inc., 1971], pp. 8-10.)

on eliminating the "export of revolution" when, for all practical purposes, this has already occurred.

6. The present policy design produces minimal short-term benefits, and long-term considerations dictate that Cuba be brought back into a more natural relationship with its neighbors, whatever its political and social systems.

7. The Castro regime can no longer be considered as temporary [2] (even in the possible absence of Castro).

8. Policy makers have come to realize that the only possible danger for the United States inherent in present circumstances resides in the potential use of Cuban territory for Russian strategic military purposes.

9. The United States no longer insists upon the removal of the communist regime in Cuba nor does it require that the Cuban government break its political, economic, and military links with the Soviet Union.

10. American officials have declared that the U. S. is prepared to be pragmatic and would be willing to *discuss* a changed relationship when and if the Cubans so desire.

For Cuba

1. Castro rhetoric notwithstanding, the Cubans have in the past implied that talks with United States would be a sensible step, although any such dialogue would perforce have to be preceded by a series of concrete, tension-reducing acts, including [3] (a) curbing armed raids by anti-Castro Cuban groups from the United States (b) lifting the U. S.-imposed trade and economic "blockade" (c) declaring a willingness to negotiate the status of the U. S. naval base at Guantánamo.

2. The Cubans may well be prepared to accept a new relationship with the United States provided its three consistent foreign policy objectives are safeguarded or perhaps enhanced as a result of the

2. The view that the Castro regime was a temporary phenomenon significantly conditioned and justified the early structuring of the U. S. anti-Castro containment policy. Former Secretary of State Dean Rusk stated, for example:
"There will be no retreat from our policy toward the Castro regime in Cuba as long as it continues to threaten the security and stability of other nations in the hemisphere. Moreover, we regard the regime as temporary." (from "Our Foreign Policy," *Vital Speeches* [March 1, 1964], p. 293.)
3. These conditions were indicated by Cuban Foreign Ministry officials in an interview with a U. S. journalist. (See *The Washington Post*, November 3, 1971, p. A26.)

77

agreement—(1) Cuba's independence (2) the preservation of the revolution (3) support for the prosecution of its developmental goals.

For the Soviet Union

1. Although the continuation of non-provocative tensions between the United States and Cuba favors Soviet goals and intentions in the hemisphere, there is little the Soviets could do to prevent a Castro initiative in seeking to improve relations with the United States.

2. Indeed, there are strong indications that the Soviet Union would welcome a lifting of the political and economic isolation policy[4] as a means of lessening its logistic burden of supplying Cuba with the bulk of its import needs, as well as taking a considerable portion of Cuba's sugar and other exports.[5]

3. Aspects of the U. S. - U. S. S. R. efforts for an over-all détente point to arrangements that, with the acquiescence of Castro, could encourage the Soviets to favor a minimal Cuban-U. S. rapprochement.[6]

In the broadest strategic sense, the United States must today face up to two rival choices in terms of its basic orientation toward the Castro regime in Cuba: it must opt for either (1) the continuation of the policy structure directed toward the isolation of Cuba, or (2) adopt a policy which, through a progressive lessening of hostility and tensions, would aim for eventual accommodation. The judgments expressed above, if correct, seem to substantiate clearly the hypo-

4. A *Tass* commentary touching on this subject stated:
"The wide movement for normalization of relations with Cuba that spread in the Western Hemisphere causes extreme irritation in Washington circles ...they refuse to reconcile themselves to the bankruptcy of their policy of isolation of Cuba and now resort to every means to make Latin American countries continue to follow their anti-Cuban course."
(See *The Washington Post*, December 22, 1971, p. A9.)

5. Sugar represents 85 % of Cuba's exports, nickel about 10 %, with tobacco, fish, and meat making up the remaining 5 %.

6. An example of this is a proposed wide-ranging U. S.-U. S. S. R. shipping agreement now in its preliminary stages (1972). According to one of its provisions, the United States would permit Soviet vessels departing from Cuban ports to pick up cargo at U. S. ports (see *The Washington Post*, April 28, 1972, p. A16). At present, as part of the over-all anti-Cuban economic denial policy, *any* ship carrying cargo to or from Cuba is black-listed and prohibited from visiting U. S. ports or carrying U. S. goods. The implications, then, of the approval of a Soviet-American agreement containing such a provision would be unmistakable: ir would represent a *de facto* first step toward a unilateral dismantlement of the denial policy, for at that point the U. S. could hardly sustain the applicability of its enforcement measures in terms of ships of other foreign registry.

thesis that the U. S. adoption of a more accommodative policy toward Cuba can no longer be ignored. A policy of accommodation would be a constructive alternative to the present anti-Castro containment policy, a legacy of prior attitudes and circumstances no longer pertinent and at variance with existing circumstances.

Yet, in actions and words, neither the United States nor Cuba has demonstrated a genuine interest in a modified relationship based on self-respect and a reconciliation of mutual interests. In some manner, then, the agressive, hostile, stereotyped views upheld by both sides must be altered in order to allow for movement toward political accommodation. In such circumstances, the American President must gauge his reading of the public temper with the possible benefits and risks of pursuing a new policy direction or continuing the status quo. Castro, in establishing priorities and aims, would be likewise required to set these against perceived changes in the over-all political context before moving to modify current relationships.

At present, both Cuba and the United States have indicated that the all-important first conciliatory gesture must come from the adversary. Given the hostility pattern that has vitiated the relationship between the two countries for over a decade, national dignity, if nothing else, seems to demand that this be so. Certainly Castro, for prestige and the maintenance of revolutionary objectives, could hardly be expected to capitulate openly to U. S. demands, while the United States similarly would need to demonstrate that it had not given in to Castro free of cost. Additionally, inasmuch as the American executive operates within a democratic political framework, it can be hypothesized that the *appearance* of a major gesture initiated by the opponent may well be necessary in such circumstances. All of these considerations take us back to a question alluded to earlier: namely, the extent to which, at this time and in these circumstances, each party can or should maneuver or encourage the other side to take the decisive first step.

Institutional and Attitudinal Impediments to Major Policy Departures

In the United States, any even suggested action which might be deemed indicative of a major departure from the current policy toward Cuba would most likely engender stiff resistance. This would develop within the governmental foreign affairs community, as well as from various interested publics—both foreign and domestic—outside the formal decision-making structure. Although the strength of such potential opposition is generally overestimated on most foreign affairs issues, its perceived existence does act as a constraining influence on the formulation and execution of fundamental policy innovations. The central function of any decision-making system is that of making choices; the choices made become policy outputs. Why either innovation or inaction might be the policy output at any given time depends, then, on both how a government functions and the attitudinal environment in which it operates. Despite subtle modifications in certain aspects of U. S. Cuban policy, the general tendency still remains that of inaction, an unwillingness to marshal forces away from the narrow focus of hostility and the attendant containment framework upon which the present policy has been constructed.

In the face of other more pressing and distracting policy priorities, the high-pitched opposition that accompanied the anti-Cuban hostility pattern in the early and mid-60's has long since been reduced to a generalized apathy. Except, then, for instances such as Cienfuegos—which encompassed larger strategic security interests—the absence of top-level attention and concern toward Cuba has left basic U. S. Cuban policy subject to the forces of institutional inertia. And within a multiple-constituency political environment of conflict and consensus, it is understandable why, given the momentum of the long-sustained hostility orientation, American foreign policy decision-makers would tend to view policy consistency as a virtue and to avoid prescriptions that would disturb prevailing opinion and operating patterns. Even though certain prestigeful publics might advocate policy innovations, with the existence of a fairly wide-spread consensus of opposition, positive changes in policy directions are difficult to set in motion. Moreover, in these circumstances, it is even more difficult to envision that this would emerge from within the national foreign policy bureaucracy.

Although there have been exceptions, historically the American bureaucracy has not been the producer of original, innovative suggestions in terms of major foreign policy departures. In fact, the bureaucracy is rather poorly equipped and structured to produce innovational policy suggestions: *institutionally*, since every major foreign policy problem falls partially within the domain of several agencies and operating offices, there is no single focal point—except at the highest policy levels—with a capability, as well as a responsability, for grasping the total dimensions and ramifications of a given problem; *individually*, there is inevitably a tendency on the part of foreign affairs officials, characteristic of all bureaucrats, to dismiss outright suggested changes which *in their opinion* would be considered unwise or unworkable by higher-level policy makers; and *motivat-*

ionally, when misjudgment can seriously impair career advancement, few officials are willing to advocate courses of action or policy positions for which support is not already clearly evident.

The point to be made here is that there is a clear tendency observable in the American foreign policy decision-making process for innovation to develop not within the bureaucracy but from outside through a *consensus* of respected individuals, institutions, and "attentive" publics. The resulting change in attitude is subsequently perceived by the key policy makers who adopt new policy guidelines which are only later implemented through the formal mechanisms of the foreign policy decisional process. This is not to imply that the bureaucracy—and certainly not the President—is entirely passive. Indeed, there is an interactive process at work in which elements of the bureaucracy actively foster support for new policy directions during the formative stages of the process. But, in general, the pressure for major policy innovation comes from the amalgamation of (1) forces originating outside the purely bureaucratic setting and (2) the President's assessment of the supportive political environment.

Thus, the role of the President, although circumscribed by the development of forces outside his personal control, is central to the entire process leading to major policy departures. Moreover, presidential leadership can contribute greatly to the formation of modified public preferences on long-standing foreign policy issues. Success depends, of course, on his skill in motivating and directing public sentiment toward the adoption of new analytic frameworks from which policy departures can be justified. To a certain extent presidents are prisoners of their times, but just how rigid and constraining are the limits of the *real world* which set the parameters of the possible in policy innovation? Public opinion is generally considered a hindrance to policy flexibility and initiative. Yet, in terms of Cuba, for example, there is little the President can rely upon to give him an accurate measurement of the degree to which various attentive publics and especially the general electorate may adhere to a given policy preference. He thus has considerable freedom to manipulate public opinion.

The multiplicity of constituencies and the need to accommodate a variety of different advocates in the American foreign policy decision-making process has resulted in the strengthened role of the White House. It serves now not only as a policy coordinator and resolver, but also as a policy innovator and instigator—particularly in situations where outside pressures are perceived to be sufficient to support major policy change. The trend toward a centralization of foreign policy decision-making within the structure of the President's personal White House staff has become institutionalized, and centers around the figure of Dr. Henry Kissinger as head of the National Security Council (NSC). While certain features of the National Security Council's role in foreign policy formulation and execution will undoubtedly change in the future, the idiosyncrasies of the present system have a decided bearing on the lack of policy innovation in terms of Cuba at this time.

One analyst,[7] for example, sees the operating system of the NSC today as dividing issues into two basic groups: one consists of high-priority items that Kissinger subjects to top-level analysis and upon which presidential attention is assured; the other, in contrast, consists of foreign policy problems that, since they remain submerged at lower bureaucratic levels, are largely ignored and characterized by policy drift. This in part, then, accounts for the lack of high-level treatment of the Cuban problem and gives another reason for the lack of a Cuban policy innovation emerging from the bureaucracy. The President has not seen fit to encourage the development of a major departure in U. S. Cuban policy. And, owing to the absence of independent power bases in the lower reaches of the foreign affairs bureaucracy under the present NSC decision management system, no official or group has been willing to risk proposing a radical departure from present policy norms. They know that, at present, this would most assuredly be sharply rejected.[8]

Thus, added to the still applicable hostility pattern of the past is an official U. S. attitude toward Cuba which can be characterized as indifference. The policy makers at the highest levels not only feel little public pressure for policy change, but also see little which Cuba can or does do which affects U. S. vital interests. In short, they prefer to ignore the problem completely, and for the moment do not

7. See I. M. Destler, "The Nixon NSC: Can One Man Do?" *Foreign Policy* (Winter 1971-72).

8. As part of its endeavors to assert more forcibly its constitutional role in foreign policy, the Senate Foreign Relations Committee in particular has sought to encourage enlightened attitudes in terms of U. S. Cuban policy. (See, for example, U. S. Congress, Senate, *United States Policy Towards Cuba*, Hearing Before the Senate Foreign Relations Committee, Washington: GPO, September 1971.) Although it is recognized that policy innovation is generally neither an appropriate nor effective role of Congress, the Committee's insistence upon an adequate and searching explanation of the administration's goals and objectives in terms of its Cuban policy is not only proper but very much in the national interest. Nonetheless, it is obvious that the Committee acknowledges its actions toward changing the Cuban policy are beyond its competence and power base. "After all," one Senate staff member confided, "for the Foreign Relations Committee, it is far harder to make something happen than to stop something from happening." (Quotation from personal interview, January 1972.)

wish to confront the variety of serious adjustments which would inevitably have to take place in any scenario which contemplates a more benevolent policy toward Cuba. In a sense, then, these words of President Johnson in 1964 could probably be repeated today, since they seem to embody current official sentiment:

> The problems of this hemisphere would be far more serious if Castro today sat at the councils of the OAS disrupting debate and blocking discussion, if Castro had open channels of trade and communications along which subversion and terror could flow, if his economy had been a successful model rather than a dismal warning to all his neighbors.[9]

The Chinese Antecedent: A Paradigm for Future U. S. Cuban Policy?

The dimensions and dynamics of every foreign policy problem differ and, accordingly, must be handled in distinct ways. Nevertheless, the similarity between the erstwhile U. S.-Chinese mutual hostility pattern and the adversary relationship the United States continues to maintain with Cuba would seem to provide a comparable contextual situation. By comparing the two, it may be possible to judge basic attitudes and probable operational modes.

In this respect, State Department Public Affairs official Robert J. McCloskey, for one, has stated the official position quite unequivocally: "We don't equate the situation in Cuba with the situation in China." [10] Nevertheless, the parallels are much too obvious to be ignored. And one can easily visualize at some point in the future a type of initiative whose quest for normalizing relations with Cuba might be justified, as with China, on a similar need to end the historical aberration of a senseless diplomatic divorce.

Several critics have, of course, already recognized the analogy between the Chinese and Cuban cases and voiced a concerned judgment. Senator George McGovern, among others, has stated that it would be foolish to establish a diplomatic dialogue with China yet "ignore a little communist country in our own backyard." [11] But, for the general public, the very size and importance of China alone—in contrast with a small and weak Cuba—do make for a more compelling argument in stressing the need for shifting away from the mainten-

9. Lyndon B. Johnson, "Our World Policy," *Vital Speeches* (May 1964), p. 420.
10. *The Times of the Americas*, December 22, 1971, p. 1.
11. *The Washington Post*, December 28, 1971, p. 1.

83

ance of a mutual hostility pattern with all its attendant policy ramifications.[12]

In the case of China, then, the clear visibility of several important U. S. interests contributed considerably to the ease by which the Nixon administration was able to garner support for a major policy departure. Any analogous effort in terms of Cuba will, however, be exceedingly difficult. Owing to the existence of several special problems in the Cuban case,[13] basic resolution will involve much more than, as in the case of China, a mere common recognition that mutual interests would be better served by the restoration of more normal relations. At present, the apparent official desire not to arouse public interest in Cuba effectively postpones the confrontation of these and other problems. This means that any benefits that might evolve from a changed U. S.-Cuban relationship are removed from the arena of widespread public consideration. Thus, a concern for the long-range implications and consequences of the continuation of the present policy toward Cuba remains restricted to a select and interested public.

Nonetheless, certain statements made by key officials seem to confirm the suspicion that the Chinese example may have a certain applicability to official attitudes toward Cuba. President Nixon himself, in answering a question (on October 12, 1971) about his proposed official visit to the Soviet Union in May 1972, indicated that it would be "possible" that he might discuss Cuba with the Russians.[14] Moreover, shortly thereafter (on October 21, 1971) Deputy Secretary of Defense Packard asserted, in terms of the possibility that the "era of negotiations" might be extended to Cuba, that this too "would be a logical move at some point."[15]

Such indications remain, of course, very much at variance with the policy statements of both the American and Cuban governments, with Castro expressing an even greater degree of intransigence than

---

12. This was a major point made by the Nixon administration for general public consumption, particularly in the early stages of its efforts to condition public opinion toward acceptance of a new policy line toward China. Secretary of State William P. Rogers stated, for example, in March 1971:

President Nixon shares this hope...that we could improve our relations with Communist China. It doesn't make sense for a nation of that size —800 million people—to be outside the world community. They have the opportunity to become active and to become involved."

(from *Department of State Bulletin* [March 29, 1971], p. 445.)

13. See the following chapter for a discussion of the major problems affecting reconciliation.

14. *The Washington Post*, October 31, 1971, p. A18.

15. *Ibid.*

the United States. A partial explanation for the stronger invective from Cuba during the Nixon administration may well have been a question of Castro's animosity against Richard M. Nixon on a personal level. For certainly it must be difficult for Castro to forget Nixon's active participation in the formulation of the Eisenhower administration's hostile posture toward the revolutionary regime. He also remembers his personal meeting with Nixon in 1959, and a number of past references by the ex-President, which include having called Castro a "madman." In his speeches, Castro often inveighed against the figure of Nixon as the American political leader, and the official Cuban newspaper *Gramma* not only incessantly called him a "fascist butcher," but also invariably used a swastika in place of "x" in printing his name.

What effect such personal attacks have cannot be known with any degree of exactness. There are strong indications, however, that Castro's penchant for vituperation and his deliberate baiting of the United States weigh heavily on U. S. official attitudes. The Russians and Chinese often say basically the same things, but somehow Castro's insolence grates more sharply on American sensitivities. Therefore, a lowering of the asperity level of Castro rhetoric would seem imperative for the creation of a climate favorable to rapprochement.

Based on the foregoing discussion, it has been asserted that the President, within broad limits, has considerable latitude for basic policy innovation. If true, the question then becomes what method would more likely be employed in making overtures to Cuba when the President decides the time is right to signal the opponent of America's altered intentions. There are three basic alternatives: (1) capitulation (2) massive conciliation, consisting of openly declared and active, unilateral initiatives [16] (3) incremental revisionism, which envisions a species of co-operation based on a series of modest, tentative steps toward full accommodation. It is here where the Chinese antecedent can perhaps illuminate the probable course of

16. What I have in mind here are proposals made by such people as phychologist C. E. Osgood (*Alternative to War or Surrender* [Urbana, Ill.: University of Illinois Press, 1962]), who calls for a deliberate "peace offensive" as a means of reducing fear and distrust between countries in antagonistic opposition. His advocated method—called "Graduated Reciprocation in Tension-Reduction" (GRIT)—requires one side to take the initiative in creating a climate for reciprocation through a series of planned, widely-publicized, unilateral acts which are executed without prior commitment by the opponent for reciprocation. Although Osgood's proposal is specifically addressed to the cold war contention between the superpowers, the basic configuration of the problem he attempts to resolve seems equally pertinent to any situation in which a hard-core mutual hostility pattern characterizes relations between nations. It is highly unlikely, however, that the Ford administration would resort to this method.

action the United States would follow once the President decided national interests dictate a move in this direction.

As a model, the Chinese case clearly indicates an incremental approach in seeking rapprochement with the Cuban revolutionary regime. Therefore, although the business of tracing the exact chronology and circumstances by which the Nixon administration managed to break down the mutual hostility pattern with the Chinesse regime must be left to a more detailed treatment by others, available information suggests a pattern of movements pertinent perhaps to predicting future behavior: [17]

(1) Most important was an action taken by President Nixon on February 1, 1969, his twelfth day in office. At that time he sent a memorandum to Dr. Henry Kissinger requesting that the National Security Council undertake a study to explore every possible avenue for developing a more friendly attitude toward and possible relations with Communist China.

(2) The initial results of this study were guidelines that stressed that nothing should be done which might encourage a specific rebuff from China nor cause a disturbing public reaction in the United States.

(3) It was also decided that the only impression to be created should be that, if and when the Chinese decided it was in their interest to respond, the United States would be prepared to indicate a corresponding positive interest.

(4) By July an inter-agency study group had also completed a list of possible suitable actions designed to signal America's new intentions and attitudes toward China. Accordingly, several low-risk initiatives were implemented, the most significant being the elimination of passport restrictions for Americans wishing to travel to China and a partial lifting of the embargo on Chinese imports and the export of non-strategic items to China.

(5) Implicit in the American position was the determination that accommodation should not be accomplished completely "free of cost" to the Chinese.

The strategy employed by the Nixon administration proved fruitful; the Chinese responded to the American initiatives by first inviting, in a symbolic gesture, an American table tennis team to China. This marked the initial step in the process that eventually led to the American President's historic visit to China in early 1972.

17. A particularly penetrating and perceptive analysis of this point is provided by journalist John Osborne in "Signals to Mao," *New Republic* (May 1, 1971), pp. 15-16.

The Chinese example may well contain some valuable clues to the American approach for resolving its Cuban problem. But the absence of several essential ingredients in the attitudinal and circumstantial mixture has precluded the initiation of the process at this time. First and foremost of these is the lack of any concrete evidence that the government is engaged in any preliminary study aimed at thoroughly examining the goals of its present Cuban policy. This would be a study conducted under a directive from the Chief Executive to the effect that the objective of the exercise must be to bring policy goals into line with the search for an appropriate means of developing friendly relations with Castro's Cuba. And, secondly, the United States has taken no specific low-risk actions which might represent a signal to Castro of its serious intentions to work toward a basic settlement.

Conclusion: The Persistence of Goal Ambiguities

Implicit in the foregoing discussion is the proposition that any fundamental modification in the prevailing mutual hostility pattern between Cuba and the United States may be impossible without the contemplation of some unilateral initiatives. Also by implication, the thought has been advanced that the United States would be the one which could more easily bend its pride in the interest of an over-all amicable settlement of differences. This, however, is not yet deemed necessary nor desirable by the United States. Even so, in comparison with the extreme nature of several formerly-held U. S. Cuban policy objectives, present attitudes have become more realistic and flexible. These can be shown schematically:

U. S. Cuban Policy

Desired Policy Outcomes (1962-1968)	Current Official Attitude (1969-1975)
I. Inside Cuba	
1. Removal of Castro.	1. Expresses a willingness to accept the Castro regime.
2. Restoration of civil liberties. 3. Free elections and a democratic political order.	2, 3, 4. Indicates that Cuba's internal institutional arrangements and its socio-economic

87

4. Return to a capitalist economic system, modified by more responsibility and power in the public sector.

order are for Cubans to determine.

II. *Regarding the Soviet Union*

1. Cut all Soviet political, economic, and military ties with Cuba.

1. (a) Stresses the non-introduction into Cuba of all potential strategic offensive weapons systems.
   (b) Prohibits the establishment of full-scale Soviet military bases.
   (c) Ceases to object to Soviet military advisory teams or the supplying of "reasonable" quantities of conventional arms.
   (d) Ceases to object to continued Soviet-Cuban trade or Soviet economic and technical assistance.
   (e) Warns that it will use all possible means to prevent the use of Cuba as a staging area for the penetration of Soviet subversion in Latin America.

III. *Regarding Latin America*

1. Stop all forms of export of revolution from Cuba.

1. Continues unchanged.

2. Cuba reincorporated into the OAS and the inter-American system.

2. Insists that the present exclusion was a collective action; therefore, the decision to reincorporate Cuba must be made jointly.

3. Discredit the Cuban developmental model.

3. Evidences a readiness to downplay this as an underlying purpose of U.S. policy.

IV. *Regarding the United States*

1. "Effective" compensation for or full restitution of the nationalized property of U. S. citizens.	1, 2, 3. Accepts these as legitimate subjects for negotiation.
2. Reincorporation of Cuba into the U. S. preferential sugar quota system.	
3. Retention of the Guantánamo naval base.	
4. Normalization as a return to the former harmonious relationship.	4. Expresses a muted readiness to discuss the possibility of establishing a modified relationship, provided Castro demonstrates a positive interest in initiating a dialogue.

The more compromising stance has not been accompanied, however, by a clear definition of the goal or goals which are presently being sought. In essence, there has been a change in attitude without a corresponding change in supportive policy actions. If seeking accommodation were the basic goal, the containment policy framework would become unsuitable and clearly counter-productive to the attainment of the desired end. However, most of the elements of the old framework remain today securely intact. Thus, the impression is created of a policy in limbo, teetering between the weighty shibboleths of the past and a partial recognition of changed realities. But, due to an unwillingness to accept the probable consequences of a full shift, a change in policy does not move forward.

Above all, the United States can no longer assume that accommodation with the Castro regime will restore harmony to hemispheric relations. In the first place, the accommodation, when it does take place, will not be a *zero-sum* settlement with the United States fully replacing the Soviet Union; the Soviet presence will remain in Cuba. In all probability it will only mean that Cuba will occupy a distinct although not wholly separate status within the U. S. sphere-of-influence. And, secondly, such a development may well accentuate the discernible trend on the part of Latin American countries to move toward a modified status in their individual and collective relationships with

89

the United States. For example, Castro may well be right in seeing the formal organizational expression of the so-called inter-American system—the OAS—as a "cadaver". Jeremiah O'Leary, a journalist whose reporting centers on Latin American events, reflected this impression in summing up the results of a recent OAS General Assembly meeting in Washington:

> The Organization of American States has completed the two-week-long spring futility rite known as the OAS General Assembly amid the thunderous pomposity and boredom that has become the group's trademark.[18]

The inter-American system has become over the years an artificial entity unilaterally promoted by the United States; it had meaning only at the time the entire hemisphere shared common problems far removed from the scene of world politics. Today, however, Latin America and the United States pursue antagonistic basic interests: Latin America seeks solutions for its socio-economic development, while the United States looks to insuring political and military objectives pertinent to its superpower status both within and without the hemisphere. Therefore, increasingly more pertinent is the idea of "Latin Americanism"—meaning effective solidarity against the paramount power. Some Latin Americans view this as the means of overcoming U. S. preponderance in the region and the "only hope for creating an organic community for the future." [19]

An informal organization made up of all the Latin American countries—called the *Special Latin American Coordinating Committee*— has met intermittently over the past three years for the purpose of formulating common views with respect to problems affecting their relationships with the United States. The seed exists, therefore, for the continued growth of Latin American solidarity vis-à-vis the United States. This trend could well translate into efforts to bring the organizational aims of the OAS even more into line with Latin America's basic interests. In brief, what the Latins want is more U. S. assistance with less U. S. interference. This is, of course, what the Third World wants from the developed nations, and what Castro wants for Cuba.

During an official visit to the United States, Mexico's outspoken President Luis Echeverría characterized Pan-Americanism as not hav-

18. *The Times of the Americas*, May 3, 1972, p. 4.
19. Jorge Castañeda, "Pan-Americanism and Regionalism: A Mexican View," International Organization, Vol. X (1956), pp. 374-388.

ing gone beyond the stage of a "lofty idea." And, in obvious reference to American domination of the organization, he stated that the OAS "cannot be a sanctuary of out-dated principles and even less an instrument for unacceptable acquiescence."[20] Such statements suggest a more forceful "Latin Americanism" in terms of making the OAS a more effective vehicle for the pursuit of Latin America's national interests. Mexico, which is apparently taking a leading role in moving the OAS toward such ends, has never abided by the 1962 decision to banish Cuba from the organization. Referring in part to the Cuban problem, President Echeverría stated in Washington:

> It is time to reflect on the harm and risks entailed in the rigid adhesion to a supposed ideological unity.[21]

The complexity of the total hemispheric problem makes the benefits inherent in the establishment of some degree of contact with the Cuban regime now extremely difficult to perceive. For it must be seen within the context of representing merely the first turn in a set of adjustments the United States will have to make in dealing with future relationships in the region. The present indecisive policy and the lack of specific, attainable goals can, of course, continue for some time. The United States does not "need" Cuba (nor, individually, most other countries in the world) and can easily ignore it, as well as the existence of tell-tale symptoms of transformation in Latin America. It may ignore them, but at a risk.

Finally, at this point in time the still-pervasive assumption that the removal of Castro alone will solve most of the U. S.'s problems associated with Cuba should not only be questioned but perhaps banished outright.[22] Bernard Fall put it succinctly:

---

20. *The Washington Post*, June 17, 1972, p. A2.
21. *Ibid.*
22. A characteristic expression of this assumption comes from Brig. General Burton R. Brown, Deputy Assistant Director of the Defense Intelligency Agency in congressional testimony:
"If we keep the pressure on, he doesn't do well and the people get more and more dissatisfied; it certainly seems possible to me that the military might decide they have had enough and this is one thing I keep in mind... I think Castro should go—and just he alone is enough—if he should go, I think the thing would be wide open and the odds would be good that another government would, will, come back into the OAS. It might not be everything we want and certainly it won't go back to the old days, but I think that would be something...the odds would be great that we would see a government which we could work with."
(from U. S. Congress, House of Representatives, Committee on Foreign Affairs,

91

> Regardless of what happens to Castro as a person and Cuba as a country, "Castroism" as a revolutionary idea has become a permanent fixture of Latin American political life.[23]

It is only necessary to add that the "revolutionary idea" to which Fall alludes need not restrict itself to a theory of revolution or a duplication of the Cuban experience; it equally embraces such connotations as a more forceful nationalism, self-respect, and a defiant refusal to accept the submissive patterns of the past.

Communist Activities in Latin America, Hearings Before the Sub-Committee on Inter-American Affairs, Washington: GPO, 1967, p. 42.)

23. Bernard Fall, "The Third World," in Clement J. Zablocki, ed., *Sino-Soviet Rivalry: Implications for U. S. Policy* (New York: Praeger, 1966).

CHAPTER VIII

OBSTACLES TO AN EVENTUAL CUBAN-AMERICAN SETTLEMENT: SUGAR, CLAIMS, GUANTANAMO, EXILES

Any forward calculations made by American policy-makers involving a possible accommodation with the Castro regime must, perforce, take into account the implications of (1) the feasibility of Cuban sugar sales in the U.S. market (2) the massive monetary claims of U.S. citizens and corporations against the revolutionary regime (3) the possibility of a modification in the treaty status of the U.S. naval base at Guantánamo (4) the activities and influence of hundreds of thousands of Cuban refugees presently in the United States.

These factors further differentiate the U.S.-Cuban settlement problem from that which the Nixon administration faced with Communist China. The long-sustained U.S.-Chinese mutual hostility pattern was overcome thanks to a carefully calibrated conditioning of public opinion by the administration, the passage of time, and a general recognition of readjustments in world power relationships. Doubtless the process would have been made more intricate and laborious if a set of obstructions similar to the ones with Cuba had existed. As it is, the only corresponding problem of this type in the case of China was the question of claims. Although this was conveniently hushed during the initial U.S.-Chinese contacts, it too will eventually have to be resolved before any significant trade can take place between the two countries.

The intricacy of these four problems, and their bearing on the outcome of any final solution to the present U. S.-Cuban diplomatic and economic divorcement, makes each worthy of extensive study and evaluation. The following presentation attempts to elucidate the main outlines of each issue and to provide basic background information. In addition, some cautious judgments are offered regarding their importance for the present and a possibly modified U. S. Cuban policy.

Cuba, the United States, and Sugar [1]

An important link with the pre-revolutionary past is the essentially one-crop nature of today's Cuban economy. Despite Castro's ambitious and costly industrial and agricultural [2] diversification projects, sugar continues to account for approximately 85 % of Cuba's export earnings. For an economy so highly dependent upon exports, this means that the level and extent of Cuba's economic performance are largely determined by the production and foreign sales of this one product.[3]

The Cuban sugar industry, therefore, remains today as dominant in the country's economy as it was prior to the advent of the Castro regime. The difference is in Cuba's sugar trade patterns, which have been radically altered. Before, a substantial portion of Cuba's sugar production entered the United States market under a preferential quota system with price advantages, while today most of the sugar is taken by the Soviet Union, other bloc countries, and the People's Republic of China under essentially barter arrangements. The re-

1. Important informational sources are: José Álvarez Díaz, ed., *Un estudio sobre Cuba* (Coral Gables, Fla.: University of Miami Press, 1963) for statistics and a history of the impact of sugar on the economic, social, and political development of Cuba; the annual reports (*Sugar Year Book*) prepared and published by the International Sugar Council (London) for comprehensive statistics on all aspects of international sugar production, consumption, imports and exports; and Philip W. Bonsal, *Cuba, Castro, and the United States* (Pittsburgh: University of Pittsburgh Press, 1971) for a lucid, non-technical analysis of sugar in regard to the U. S.-U. S. S. R.-Cuban triangular relationship.

2. The Castro regime has invested sizeable quantities of scarce capital into such projects as rice, citrus fruit, and coffee plantations, as well as into the enlargement and qualitative improvement of livestock production (see Leo Huberman and Paul M. Sweezy, *Socialism in Cuba*, New York: Monthly Review Press, 1969, pp. 65-85).

3. See Bonsal, *Cuba, Castro, and the United States*, p. 218; U. S. Department of Commerce, *Investment in Cuba*, (Washington: Government Printing Office, 1956), p. 7; and *The Washington Post*, November 14, 1971, p. A30.

mainder is sold on the world market for prices which, until only recently, have ranged only slightly over Cuban production costs. The problem today for Cuba is not, however, an inability to sell its crop, but to increase its production to meet commitments. The Soviet Union continues to take up to 5 million tons of Cuban sugar; approximately 1.5 million tons are required under bilateral arrangements with other communist countries; a 2 million ton quota had been assigned to Cuba under the International Sugar Agreement; and .5 million tons are deemed a minimal domestic requirement under rationing conditions.[4] Even considering that Cuba has never provided the Soviet Union with more than 2.5 million tons (and in recent years only 1.5 million tons per year), a reduced commitment of 6.5 million tons represents more than the average Cuban sugar production under the Castro regime, which has been:

Cuban Sugar Production [5]
(1960-1974)

Year	Production (in tons)
1960	5,862,000
1961	6,707,000
1962	4,815,000
1963	3,821,000
1964	4,465,000
1965	6,220,000
1966	4,530,000
1967	6,340,000
1968	5,280,000
1969	4,540,000
1970	8,530,000 [6]
1971	5,800,000
1972	4,200,000
1973	5,300,000
1974	6,200,000 est.

4. Bonsal, *ibid.*, p. 211; interviews with State Department analysts, March 1972.

5. Statistics supplied by the Office of the Coordinator of Cuban Affairs, Department of State (December 1972, August 1973, and March 1974).

6. Cuba's highest production total before 1970 was 7,012,000 tons produced in 1952.

95

Although the Soviet Union pays 11 cents a pound for Cuban sugar,[7] 80 % of this is payable in Soviet goods; therefore, between this trade and barter arrangements with other socialist countries, Cuba is in the position of having to earmark three-fourths of its production for the Eastern Bloc. The Cubans are thus obligated to meet their foreign exchange needs for the purchase of essential Western imports from the sale of slightly over 2 million tons on the world market at generally depressed prices.

As a major sugar export nation, Cuba's problems would be substantial even in the absence of its present trade relationships. Today the world produces and consumes approximately 82 million tons of sugar annually (55 % cane and 45 % beet), of which 75 % is sold domestically within the producing nations, thereby leaving about 20.5 million tons for export to world markets.[8] Half of this amount is marketed under special preferential arrangements (with the U. S., the U. S. S. R., and the U. K.), leaving 10.3 million tons or 12 % of the world total subject to sale at so-called international prices—which have oscillated widely, from a low in recent years of 1.5 cents a pound in 1968 to an above average 18.5 cents a pound in early 1974.[9] Under the terms of the 1968 International Sugar Agreement (the U. S. was not a party to the agreement), Cuba was allocated a quota of 2.15 million tons.[10] As a result of this arrangement, the world sugar market stabilized considerably, with the price per pound rising to an average level of just slightly over 4 cents. Even this, however, represents a "residual," non-economic price, since the average world production cost of sugar is in the neighborhood of 5.5 cents per pound. And even with Cuba's below average production cost (4 cents per pound),[11] at best it merely broke even at that time in its international sales—the bulk of which then and now is taken by Japan.

Cuba's chief trading relationship today is with the Soviet Union.

7. The Soviets agreed to pay Cuba 11 cents per pound for its sugar export to the U. S. S. R. during the period 1973-1980. (See *San Juan Star*, January 10, 1973, p. 10.)

8. These and the following statistics are taken from A. Guy Sauzier (London), "The World Sugar Market and the International Sugar Agreement," in U. S. Congress, House of Representatives, *Extension of the Sugar Act*, Hearings Before the Committee on Agriculture, Washington: Government Printing Office, 1971, pp. 786-789 and *New York Times*, February 11, 1974, p. 53.

9. By November 1974 the world price soared to an all-time high of 60 cents a pound on the London market. It is still too early to determine if the high price—produced by the pressure of increased world demand—represents an aberration or a new permanent trend.

10. Bonsal, *Cuba, Castro, and the United States*, p. 210. The International Sugar Agreement was not extended in 1974.

11. U. S. Congress, *Extension of the Sugar Act.*, p. 647.

It is not based, however, on a mutually profitable—in strictly economic terms—arrangement. Russia supplies Cuba with most of its import needs in amounts that far exceed Cuba's capacity to pay, for which Cuba, in exchange, sends principally sugar. Nonetheless, for its own foreign policy interests and in the spirit of "socialist brotherhood," the Soviets have been willing to sustain a considerable payments imbalance which has become tantamount to the subsidization of the Cuban economy. Conservative estimates place the subsidy at the equivalent of one million dollars a day. This figure is probably far under actual amounts. But, given the dimensions of Soviet economic capability, this support to Cuba cannot be considered overly burdensome—and is dwarfed by U. S. expenditures, for example, in Vietnam. Moreover, Soviet subsidies to Cuba do not exceed the $500 million which the United States annually makes available in direct federal payments to Puerto Rico—whose 2.7 million citizens (in contrast to Cuba's population of 8.8 million) pay no federal income taxes.[12] Whatever the case, it can also be argued that, in addition to obvious political advantages, the Soviet Union does derive some strictly economic benefits from its sugar exchange with Cuba. This is stressed by Huberman and Sweezy:

> ... it is important to understand that Soviet economic policies toward Cuba, centering on the sugar agreement of 1964, are in no sense charity but on the contrary may well yield substantial long-run economic benefits to the U. S. S. R. There are several factors which combine to produce this conclusion: (1) Because of the nature of its soil and climate the Soviet Union is not and probably never will be a low-cost agricultural producer, and it is certain that it is a high-cost producer of sugar. (2) Again because of its soil and climate, but also because of historic specialization, Cuba is a low-cost producer of sugar, perhaps the lowest-cost producer in the world. (3) The Soviet Union is a low-cost producer of the things Cuba is most in need of: oil, trucks and jeeps, tractors, machinery, etc. (4) It follows that if prices are set in reasonable relation to cost, the Soviet Union can reduce the average cost of its sugar consumption by exchanging what Cuba needs for Cuban sugar. (5) Furthermore, since the Soviet Union is in the phase of economic development characterized by a rapid growth of sugar consumption, this result can be attained without endangering existing Soviet investments in the growing and processing of sugar beets: all that need be done is to slow down the rate of growth of domestic sugar production.[13]

12. *San Juan Star*, September 13, 1973, p. 6.
13. Huberman and Sweezy, *Socialism in Cuba*, pp. 77-78. Given the spectacular jump in the international price of sugar, the 11 cents per pound the Soviets pay for Cuban sugar is a bargain.

8

Historical and sentimental reasons apart, there is little question that climate and soil conditions coupled with the island's geographic location make Cuba an ample producer of high-grade, low-cost sugar whose natural market is its nearest continental neighbor—the United States. This, in fact, was the case up to the time the Eisenhower administration decided to cut off the Cuban sugar quota (in July 1960) both as a reprisal measure and as an indirect attempt to overthrow the Castro regime. For decades prior to this action Cuba had been the principal foreign purveyor of sugar to the U.S. market. And Cuba's predominant sugar import position had continued even after the passage of the Jones-Costigan Act by the U.S. Congress in 1934, the first in a series of legislative acts which have developed into what is now known as the U.S. sugar program.

Originally the legislation sought to regulate this commodity in the face of depression economic conditions. The program continued and became predicated on three basic purposes: (1) to ensure an adequate supply of sugar at "reasonable" cost (2) to maintain the domestic industry (3) to promote the export trade of the United States.[14] It will cease to exist on December 31, 1974, however, unless the American Congress is able to reach agreement on the continuing validity of the program's basic philosophy and such details as the continuation of government subsidies to growers and producers, as well as wage payments and benefits to sugar workers. During the first 26 years of the U.S. sugar program—up to 1960—Cuba supplied almost two-thirds of the foreign sugar imports (an average 2.7 million tons annually during the 1950's),[15] with most of the remainder coming from the Philippines. Although the imported sugar benefited from a preferential price which was generally at least double the prevailing world price, it can be argued that the differential did not, in the case of Cuba, constitute "aid," since, in reciprocity, Cuba had granted tariff and commercial concessions to American exporters of industrial and agricultural products. And, in fact, in most years prior to the revolution, the U.S.-Cuban trade balance was favorable to the United States.[16]

The abrupt cessation of the Cuban sugar imports in 1960 signaled the initiation of a new era in the U.S. sugar program; instead of importing mainly from Cuba and the Philippines, 35 countries have come to participate in the program.[17] Moreover, for these countries,

14. U.S. Congress, *Extension of the Sugar Act.*, p. 2.
15. Bonsal, *Cuba, Castro, and the United States*, p. 207.
16. U.S. Congress, *Extension of the Sugar Act.*, p. 647.
17. Public Law 92-138, 92nd Congress, H. R. 8866, *Sugar Act Amendments of 1971*, October 14, 1971.

there is no question that the preferential U. S. price—for example, 8.57 cents per pound in June 1971, compared with the then prevailing world price of 4.12 cents [18]—provided a profit margin which qualifies as foreign aid, since the differential entailed a transfer of resources from the United States to these countries under concessional terms. Hence, these nations have been providing 45 % of America's estimated sugar needs of 12.3 million tons annually.[19]

During the 1960's and up to the passage of the *Sugar Act Amendments of 1971*, Cuba had been allocated a "suspended" quota of 1.5 million tons,[20] or 50 % of the foreign quota apart from specified amounts for the Philippines and Ireland. This constituted the so-called "Cuban Reserve," which, in turn, was re-allocated to other—primarily Latin American—countries on a "temporary" basis. These quotas have represented important sources of foreign exchange for the countries concerned, as well as an additional foreign policy instrument which the United States has used for political advantage. For instance, when Peru under President Manuel Prado became the first Latin American nation to break relations with Castro (in 1961), the U. S. rewarded it with a 100 % increase in its U. S. sugar quota.[21] Under pressure from these foreign sugar exporters, the 1971 legislation reduced the "Cuban Reserve" from 50 % to 23.74 % of the unspecified foreign quota, or to 738,129 tons, with the difference distributed among the other foreign suppliers on a permanent basis. This major reduction was resisted by the Department of State, whose spokesman (Julius L. Katz, Deputy Assistant Secretary for International Resources and Food Policy) argued:

> While a change has no practical effect on present quotas, it does have implications for the future position of supplying countries. While we had recommended a reduction of 300,000 tons, we believe that a substantial cut, as contained in the House bill, would undermine the purpose of the reserve; that of assuring the availability to the Cuban people of an adequately beneficial sugar quota at such time as diplomatic relations with the United States are restored and the President deems such trade to be in the interest of the United States.[22]

Apparently the meaning of the preservation of a Cuban quota, and the State Department's defense of the same, is that at some point

18. U. S. Congress, Senate, *Sugar Act Amendments of 1971*, Hearings Before the Committee on Finance, Washington: Government Printing Office, 1971, p. 67.
19. *New York Times*, June 3, 1974, p. 49.
20. *Latin America* (London), Vol. V, No. 17 (April 23, 1971), p. 2.
21. *Ibid.*
22. *Department of State Bulletin* (July 19, 1971), p. 89.

Cuba will regain entry into the U.S. preferential sugar market, although at a drastically reduced level from the norm prevailing prior to the revolution. Thus, from the above statement alone, it could be argued that the United States has not expected the revolution to collapse into complete chaos, and that a more likely eventuality will be a gradual and partial re-establishment of trade and commercial relations between the two countries. The reduction in the "Cuban Reserve" not only seemed to reflect the realization that Cuban-U.S. relations had been unalterably changed, but also fixed a sugar trade arrangement which only with great difficulty would be able to be readjusted to the traditional U.S.-Cuban economic relationship.

The question of a resumption of Cuban sugar sales to the United States would also be inhibited—or at least conditioned—by the existence of an associated problem: the issue of massive U.S. claims against the Cuban government. But, even with a solution to the latter problem, in what manner would reinstatement of Cuban sugar sales most likely take place? From the standpoint of U.S. domestic suppliers, the general view seems to be that, to avoid serious disruptions, Cuba should be given a share of the market growth, but only a share of that growth allocated to foreign suppliers. This would continue until such time as the amount progressively reached the assigned level reflected in current legislation.[23]

The policy most frequently recommended is that once Cuba again becomes a supplier to the United States, it should be given a 50 % share of the foreign growth quota. At present growth rates, the official estimate is that U.S. sugar needs will increase by 230,000 tons per year.[24] Thus, the amount of this increase available for allocation to foreign suppliers would be around 75,000 tons per year. If Cuba, then, were given 50 % of this amount, it would take almost 20 years to reach the Cuban quota level under the 1971 legislation, which, in itself, represents less than 25 % of the amount the country supplied prior to 1960. Present foreign suppliers will also undoubtedly balk at any attempt to assign Cuba a sizeable amount of the foreign growth rate, since they will want an increased share for themselves. In fact, however, Section 202 (e) of Public Law 89-331 (1965), provides that "whenever the President finds it is no longer contrary to the national interest to reestablish a quota...the entire amount of such quota shall be restored for the third full calendar year following such finding by

23. See *ibid.*, pp. 50, 59, and 95. This assumes that some type of sugar quota system will be retained.
24. U.S. Congress, *Sugar Act Amendments of 1971*, p. 42. Sugar consumption in the United States has remained constant for decades at an annual rate of about 100 pounds per capita. (See *New York Times*, June 3, 1974, p. 49.)

the President." Nevertheless, in practical terms, the existence of the vocal foreign and domestic sugar constituency will add to the problem of restoring some type of normal trade relationship with Cuba—whatever regime might be in control there.

Between the uncertainty of international sugar prices and the current absence of a stable U. S. sugar program, the question of Cuban sugar reentering the American market is becoming a question of some public concern. And no viable alternative U. S. policy toward Cuba can be considered without taking into account this extremely important issue.

U. S. Claims Against the Cuban Government

Any future over-all U. S. settlement with Cuba, whether with Castro or some other regime, will depend to a large extent upon the manner in which the problem of claims against the Cuban government is resolved. This is a crucial issue, for it is one that is directly linked to the question of sugar trade, as well as, indeed, the type of relationship the United States is prepared to establish with Cuba.

The distinguishing characteristic of the Cuban claims issue—in comparison with U. S. claims, either past or pending, against other nations—is its very magnitude. Although reduced through pre-adjudication procedures, U. S. nationals have filed 8816 claims, for a total *asserted* amount of $3,346,406,271.36 against the Cuban government.[25] This sum not only represents more than the amount expropriated by all other communist governments combined [26] (U. S. S. R., Poland, Rumania, Czechoslovakia, Hungary, Yugoslavia, and Bulgaria), but also indicates the extent of direct U. S. involvement in the Cuban economy prior to the Cuban revolution.

The basis of these claims rests on the U. S. contention that, as a result of various actions by the Castro regime during 1959 and 1960, the Cuban government violated international law in seizing most of the property of American nationals (except for the U. S. naval base at Guantánamo) without provision for payment of "adequate, effective, and prompt" [27] compensation. That private property cannot be

25. *Summary of the Cuban Claims Program—Final Decisions (As of June 30, 1972),* provided by the staff of the Foreign Claims Settlement Commission, Washington, D. C. (January, 1973).

26. Sidney Friedberg, "The Measure of Damages in Claims Against Cuba," *Inter-American Economic Affairs,* Vol. XXIII., No. 1 (Summer 1969), p. 72.

27. First used by Secretary of State Hull in his note to the Mexican Government of August 22, 1938 (see Department of State Press Release, August 25, 1938).

taken without just compensation reflects a strict adherence to the traditional standards of international law. There are, however, other legal views on this still unsettled question. One, resorted to by Cuba in defense of its actions, asserts that only "equality of treatment" is required. This is interpreted as meaning that nationalization without compensation is licit so long as both foreigners and nationals are afforded the same treatment. Still another view suggests that only partial compensation is required.[28]

The Castro government had seized sizeable amounts of U. S.-owned property before the United States government cut off the Cuban sugar quota. The properties were taken in accord with the so-called *Law of Nationalization*, which was decreed on July 6, 1960. A provision for compensation in 30-year bonds at 2 % interest was contained in the decree-law. Although never implemented, the provision provided for payment through the creation of a special fund to which contributions would come from the sale of sugar to the U. S. market—but only after Cuban sales exceeded 3.5 million tons annually at a minimum price of 5.75 cents per pound. Until sales reached this level and price, no payment of principal or interest would be made on the bonds. The practical effect of this provision was the effective non-payment of all nationalized properties, for it was contingent upon the attainment of sales to the U. S. market at volume and price levels far in excess of those prevailing at the time. Since then, the U. S. price has surpassed this stipulated level, but it is unlikely that the Cuban sugar quota would have been augmented much beyond its then current level of 3.2 million tons.[29]

U. S. indignation at Castro's wholesale nationalization of U. S. properties has not yet subsided, and understandably so, since seizures of this type involve a fundamental principle of international law which the United States wishes to uphold for the protection of its economic interests throughout the world. The U. S. government investment guarantee program now available to U. S. investors overseas came into being a year before the Castro takeover in Cuba (that is, on November 29, 1957), but since it was not available for existing investment, the program offered no financial protection for U. S. investments

This language represents official U. S. policy today in regard to all instances involving the nationalization of American property in foreign countries.

28. See Edward D. Re, "The Foreign Claims Settlement Commission and International Claims," *Syracuse Law Review*, Vol. 13, No. 4 (Summer 1962), p. 517.

29. U. S. Congress, House of Representatives, *U. S. Sugar Program*, Study Prepared for the House Committee on Agriculture, Washington, Government Printing Office, 1970, p. 19.

already in Cuba.[30] Thus, practically all U. S. investments in Cuba were affected, including that of the U. S. government which directly owned the Moa Bay Mining Company (nickel), purportedly worth $100 million.[31]

Four years after the actual seizures, President Lyndon B. Johnson expressed the prevailing U. S. attitude by offering the view that these actions had "violated every standard by which the nations of the free world conduct their affairs." [32] Nonetheless, he was seemingly optimistic that the U. S. containment policy would be effective in the eventual elimination of Castro, whereupon the new government that emerged would settle the claims question amicably and fairly. He stated:

> I am confident that the Cuban people will not always be compelled to suffer under communist rule—that one day they will achieve freedom and democracy. I am also confident that it will be possible to settle the claims of American nationals whose property has been wrongfully taken from them.[33]

Traditionally, there have been four methods of settlement in situations involving claims against foreign governments: [34]

(1) *Remedy Through Diplomatic Channels.* All the various methods depend, initially, upon diplomacy, for it is only through diplomatic discourse that a particular method of settling claims disputes can be agreed upon by two or more nations. The diplomatic method *per se*, however, generally proves cumbersome for dealing with large numbers of individual claims.

(2) *Recourse to the Courts of the Nationalizing Country.* This method's weakness is obvious. Large-scale confiscations generally take place within an unsettled and volatile political setting. It is likely, therefore, that in such conditions the courts of the nationalizing country would not be a wholly objective forum for foreign claims settlements. Moreover, in any case, the outsider will always be wary of "justice" that is dispensed by a foreign court.

30. U. S. Congress, House of Representatives, *Claims of U. S. Nationals Against the Government of Cuba,* Hearings Before the Sub-Committee on Inter-American Affairs, Committee on Foreign Affairs, Washington: Government Printing Office, 1964, p. 42.

31. *Ibid.,* p. 44.

32. Quoted in Edward D. Re, "The Foreign Claims Settlement Commission and the Cuban Claims Program," article reprint from *The International Lawyer,* Vol. 1, No. 1 (October 1966), p. 4.

33. *Ibid.*

34. See Re, "The Foreign Claims Settlement Commission and International Claims," pp. 517-519.

(3) *The Mixed Claims Commission.* This is generally an *ad hoc* tribunal whose membership includes various nationalities—or only the parties directly involved. The disputing nations agree to respect the decisions on all individual claims rendered by this body. The method has its limitations, particularly its lack of any enforcement machinery; any case of non-compliance would mean a return to traditional diplomatic channels for redress of grievances. There is also a tendency in this method for the commission's membership to vote along national political lines without regard to true justice and equity.

(4) *Lump-Sum Payment.* Here, through diplomacy, the contending parties agree to a specific lump-sum payment to cover the totality of claims. The decisions over how this sum is applied to and divided among the various claimants is then determined by the judicial machinery of the payee country on the basis of its own criteria and rendered by its own judges. This is the more common method utilized today in international settlement cases, although funds may come from such alternative sources as the liquidation of foreign assets in the payee's country.

In dealing with the question of its claims against the government of Cuba, the United States established a new technique in international claims settlement—the *pre-settlement adjudication of claims.* The procedure became operational upon the enactment of H. R. 12259 —passed by Congress on October 2, 1964 and signed by President Johnson on October 16, 1964—which became Public Law 88-666, Title V of the International Claims Settlement Act of 1949, As Amended [78 Stat. 1110].[35] The newly added Title V authorized the Foreign Claims Settlement Commission to determine the amount and validity of claims against the Cuban government, but specifically precluded any authorization for payment of such claims.[36] Hence, the pre-adjudication of claims technique was established to provide an accurate record of these claims, "while witnesses, memories, and records are still available and reliable," as an aid in enhancing the possibility that a just and adequate settlement can result from any future negotiations on the question with the Cuban government.[37]

An earlier version of this legislation had provided for payment from the proceeds of vested property blocked in the United States

35. See U. S. Congress, *Legislation on Foreign Relations With Explanatory Notes,* the Committee on Foreign Relations, Senate, and the Committee on Foreign Affairs, House of Representatives, Washington: Government Printing Office, April 1971, pp. 1042-1076.
36. *Ibid.,* Section 501 of Title V, p. 1072.
37. U. S. Congress, *Claims of U. S. Nationals Against the Government of Cuba,* p. 18.

under the *Cuban Assets Control Regulations* of July 8, 1963. This provision was excluded for two reasons: on the one hand, the administration opposed the vesting of foreign property—except as reparation for war claims—on the basis that it would be contrary to national policy and, moreover, that this would be tantamount to similar unlawful seizure; [38] and, on the other hand, a census conducted by the Treasury Department showed that the amount available from blocked assets would be trivial—just over $60 million, of which only $2.5 million corresponded to the assets of the Cuban government. [39]

The Foreign Claims Settlement Commission (FCSC) [40] was thus empowered by this legislation to undertake the task of determining the amount and validity of U.S. claims against the Cuban government, based upon: "(1) debts for merchandise furnished or services rendered by nationals of the United States (2) losses arising since January 1, 1959 as a result of the nationalization or other taking of property belonging to U.S. nationals and (3) disability or death of nationals of the United States resulting from actions taken by, or under the authority of, the Government of Cuba since January 1, 1959." [41] Although fundamentally a judicial body, the FCSC does not actually "settle" claims, it merely certifies awards. Actual settlement is accomplished by the Department of State in conjunction with the Department of the Treasury, the latter authorized to make payments in accord with established limitations and priorities. [42]

The Cuban Claims Program of the FCSC began on May 1, 1965 and, by legislation, ended on July 6, 1972—although it is expected that at some later date U.S. nationals who are now in Cuba and unable to file a claim will be permitted to do so when conditions make it feasible. [43] The Cuban Program is now complete. Statistics supplied by the Commission show that it had received and processed a total of 8,816

38. *Ibid.*, pp. 45 and 137.
39. *Ibid.*, pp. 161-162.
40. The Foreign Claims Settlement Commission is the twentieth national claims commission established by the United States government. Its existence dates from 1954, at which time the functions of two earlier commissions—the International Claims Commission, administering claims under the International Claims Settlement Act of 1949, and the War Claims Commission, administering claims under the War Claims Act of 1948—were combined and transferred to the FCSC (see *ibid*).
41. Foreign Claims Settlement Commission of the United States, *Annual Report to the Congress of the United States, January 1 - December 30, 1970*, Washington: Government Printing Office, 1971, p. 10.
42. Edward D. Re, "The Foreign Claims Settlement Commission and the Cuban Claims Program," p. 13.
43. From an interview with a FCSC lawyer (January 1972).

claims (an additional 1710 were dismissed without consideration by the Commission or withdrawn).[44] Of this number, 1,146 represented claims of U. S. corporations asserting losses of $2.865 billion, while 7,670 claims were filed by individual U. S. citizens for an asserted value of $490.4 million. Thus, the *asserted* value of losses sustained through Cuba's nationalization of U. S. properties was $3.346 billion. Below is a more comprehensive statistical analysis:[45]

Cuban Claims Program—Final Decisions

	Number	Amount	Amount Claimed
Awards	5911	$1,799,546,568.69 [46]	$1,799,548,568.69
Denials	1195		1,546,857,702.67
Total	8816	1,799,546,568.69	3,346,406,271.36
Awards to Corporations	898	1,578,498,839.55	
Awards to Individuals	5013	221,049,729.14	

Analysis of Awards

Amounts of Awards	To Corporations	To Individuals	Total
$1,000 or less	63	1252	1313
1,001 to 5,000	195	1701	1896
5,001 to 10,000	100	640	740
10,001 to 25,000	134	593	727
25,001 to 50,000	89	328	417
50,001 to 100,000	51	208	259
100,001 to 250,000	77	145	222
250,001 to 500,000	56	74	130
500,001 to 1,000,000	92	39	131
Total	898	5013	5911

44. *Cuban Program Summary*, supplied by the staff of the FCSC, Washington, D. C. (January 1973).

45. *Ibid.*

46. This represents the aggregate principal; it thus excludes interest at the rate of six percent per annum from the date of the respective losses to whenever the claims may be settled by agreement between the governments of Cuba and the United States. (Letter of October 12, 1972 to the author from Francis T. Masterson, Executive-Director, Foreign Claims Settlement Commission.)

The most significant aspect of this tally is the amount of certified awards corresponding to U. S. corporations ($1.58 billion) in comparison with that of individual claimants ($221 million). Further statistical evidence discloses the extent to which Cuba is in debt to certain individual American companies or consortiums of U. S. firms: [47]

Ten Highest Certifications of Loss
Under the Cuban Claims Program

Climant		Award
1. Cuban Electric Company		$267,568,413.62
2. International Telephone and		
Telegraph Corporation		130,679,758.02
3. North American		
Sugar Industries, Inc.	$97,373,414.72	
Cuban-American		
Mercantile Corporation	52,688.46	
West Indian Company	11,548,959.95	
		108,975,063.13
4. Moa Bay Mining Company		88,349,000.00
5. United Fruit Sugar Company		85,110,147.00
6. West Indies Sugar Company		84,880,957.55
7. American Sugar Company		81,011,240.24
8. Standard Oil Company		71,611,002.90
9. Bangor Punta Corporation	39,078,904.64	
Baragua Industrial Corporation	6,280,722.17	
Florida Industrial Corporation		
of New York	3,749,751.18	
Macareno Industrial Corporation		
of New York	4,145,316.01	
Bangor Punta Operations	124,429.06	
		53,379,123.06
10. Texaco Inc.		50,081,109.67

The losses sustained by certain U. S. corporations and individuals are huge by any standard. But little known is the degree to which most of these very same companies and individuals have benefited from U. S. federal tax provisions to minimize the financial effects of such losses—an expedient not available to those whose limited income

47. *Cuban Program Summary.*

does not permit extensive write-offs for property losses. No comprehensive study has been done on the question of what percentage of the corporate or individual losses has been subtracted from tax payments to the U.S. government. It seems likely, however, that thus far the American taxpayer, and not the individuals or corporations with large official claims, has been the real loser in Cuba.

A case in point to support the above contention is the claim of the American and Foreign Power Company, Inc., whose Cuban subsidiary, the Cuban Electric Company (which supplied 90 % of all electricity sold in Cuba prior to its expropriation in 1960), presently holds the highest certified claim in dollar value against the Cuban government —$267,568,413.62. An examination of the company's financial report for 1967 revealed this highly pertinent and telling statement:

> The company and its U.S. incorporated subsidiaries file a consolidated U.S. federal income tax return. Because of tax deductibility of losses resulting from the seizure of Cuban properties in August, 1960, it is expected that no federal income taxes will be payable for the years 1960-67. However, a provision in lieu of U.S. federal income taxes equivalent to the tax benefits of such losses has been made ongoing income with a corresponding credit to the Investment Reserve.[48]

In 1968, the American and Foreign Power Company merged with Ebasco, and the latter was able to carry forward the tax deductible benefits of the absorbed company. Referring to foreign property losses, the paragraph below appeared in the annual financial report of Ebasco:

> As a result of the merger, it is expected that no U.S. income taxes will be payable by Ebasco Industries, Inc. and its U.S.-incorporated subsidiaries for the year 1968 in the fixing of a consolidated U.S. income tax return.[49]

Ebasco later merged with Boise Cascade Corporation, and it can be assumed that the latter continues to benefit from the "losses" sustained by the original Cuban Electric Company.[50] However, should this

48. American and Foreign Power Company, Inc., *Financial Report*, 1967, p. 10.
49. Ebasco Industries, Inc., *Financial Report*, 1968, p. 8.
50. Interestingly, Boise Cascade Corporation is likewise the heir of the largest certified claim against the Chinese Communist regime. It picked up 80 % of Shanghai Power's stock when it merged with Ebasco. Shanghai Power had supplied electricity to the International Settlement in that city. The FCSC certified award to this company is $ 53,832,885 (see *Business Week*, February 12, 1972, p. 16).

company (as well as all companies or persons taking such deductions) receive compensation for or the restitution of its Cuban properties, an appropriate payment of federal taxes would be required.

The settlement of the claims question with Cuba could be resolved by (1) the return of properties (with compensation given for damages and depreciation) (2) the payment of compensation (3) a combination of restitution and compensation (4) full or token lump-sum payment (5) a negotiated agreement for gradual restitution and/or compensation (probably partial) (6) complete cancellation of these debt claims, resulting in actual financial losses only to small, individual claimants, although the U. S. government could agree to pay or offer tax credits to these individuals to offset the tax benefits already given to the big corporations and large individual claimants. The alternative followed will quite obviously depend upon the willingness, capacity, and nature of the Cuban government which comes to settlement terms with the United States.

Past experience shows that most claims settlements are partial, and usually paid from blocked assets or through negotiated lump-sum payments. The Polish Agreement of 1960, for example, provided for a lump-sum payment of $40 million over a 20-year period beginning in January 1961. Approved awards in this case totaled, however, $100,736,781, which means that only about 36 % of the total amount certified will be *eventually* paid.[51] Even the Soviet Union paid only $8.6 million against the approved awards of $70.57 million for U. S. claims against the communist regime prior to 1933. This amount was agreed to in the *Litvinov Assignments* of October 25, 1953. Compensation from liquidated assets in the United States has, in most cases, also been minimal. For example, 1135 approved awards in the Hungarian Program totaled $58,181,408 while the vesting of assets provided only $1,653,647 with which to pay the certified claims.

Inasmuch as all the prior claims settlement cases involved far lesser amounts, the prospects of compensation for the holders of Cuban awards are indeed dim. Even in the unlikely case of Cuba's return to a *status quo ante*, the restitution of properties would be exceedingly difficult and payment would still have to be made for damages and depreciation. Moreover, it is probable that any new government in Cuba, even under a resuscitated capitalist economic system, would be reluctant—if not politically unable—to return such

---

51. These and the following statistics come from the *Claims Programs Under the International Claims Settlement Act of 1949, As Amended: Programs Under Title I, Program Summary Sheet*, Foreign Claims Settlement Commission, Washington, D. C., January 1972.

properties as major public utilities and refining facilities. Neither of these possibilities would be feasible, of course, so long as Castro is in power.

Whatever the case, Cuba's compensation payments could come only from the sale of its sugar. Therefore, should an arrangement be concluded whereby payment for compensation would come from the premium over world prices received from its sugar sales to the American market—as has been suggested—the result would be that the U. S. taxpayer and consumer would be paying off the Cuban debts to U. S. corporations and individuals.[52] And even this would depend on the extent to which the U. S. sugar quota could be manipulated to provide placement for Cuban sugar up to its present prescribed amount—minimal by pre-revolutionary standards—under the so-called "Cuban Reserve."

Indications are that very little, if any, thought is presently being given by the U. S. government to how it proposes to resolve the Cuban claims issue. Policy makers see it—and rightfully so—as intimately linked to the political questions of when and with what government in Cuba the United States will be prepared to establish a dialogue. It exists, however, as a very important obstacle to rapprochement.

Guantánamo: Its Political, Military, and Legal Status

Perhaps the most anomalous aspect of contemporary U. S.-Cuban relations, given the enmity and distrust between the two nations, is the continued existence of a U. S. military installation within Cuban territory. The Guantánamo Naval Base—known affectionately as "Gitmo" by old Navy hands and referred to as *Caimanera* by the Cubans —stands today as the last remaining symbol of the U. S.'s traditional relationship with Cuba. But, as Castro puts it:

> There is a base on our island territory directed against Cuba and the revolutionary government of Cuba, in the hands of those who declare themselves enemies of our country, enemies of our revolution, and enemies of our people.[53]

52. It has been estimated that if Cuba could regain its former, pre-revolutionary U. S. sugar quota (approximately three million tons annually) and place the entire amount of the premium over the world price in a special fund, it would have the capacity to pay $ 100 million a year toward the compensation of seized properties (see U. S. Congress, *Claims of U. S. Nationals Against the Government of Cuba*, p. 49).

53. Quoted in Martin Kenner and James Petras, eds., *Fidel Castro Speaks* (N. Y.: Grove Press, Inc., 1969), p. 32.

Thus, its presence is not desired by the Cubans, only tolerated, owing to the lack of a means or a capacity to remove this vestige of *Americana* from their soil.

The Castro regime has repeatedly insisted that the United States return the territory occupied by the Guantánamo base to Cuba, and the revolutionary regime has always included the question of the "illegal" occupation of Guantánamo in its lists of demands which must be met before any negotiation contemplating a normalization of relations can be initiated. This has never been an issue of central importance for Cuba, but unquestionably the status of the base will figure in any agenda of matters to be resolved before major links can be forged between the two countries.

Officially, the U. S. position on the Guantánamo issue has wavered only slightly from this Presidential statement made on November 1, 1960:

> While the position of the Government of the United States with respect to the naval base at Guantánamo has, I believe, been made very clear, I would like to reiterate it briefly: Our rights in Guantánamo are based on international agreements with Cuba and include the exercise of complete jurisdiction and control over the area. These agreements with Cuba can be modified or abrogated by agreement between the two parties, that is, the United States and Cuba. Our government has no intention of agreeing to a modification or abrogation of these agreements and will take whatever steps that may be appropriate to defend the base. The people of the United States, and all the peoples of the world, can be assured that the U.S. presence in Guantánamo and the use of that base pose no threat whatever to the sovereignty of Cuba, to the peace and security of its people, or to the independence of any of the American countries. Because of its importance to the defense of the entire hemisphere, particularly in the light of the intimate relations which now exist between the present government of Cuba and the Sino-Soviet bloc, it is essential that our position in Guantánamo be clearly understood.[54]

Cuba, on the other hand, early argued that it was not only dangerous to have a U. S. base in the "heart" of its national territory in the event of a war between the United States and Russia,[55] but also that it feared the United States might use the base as an excuse to

---

54. *Department of State Bulletin*, November 21, 1960, p. 780.
55. See R. Hart Phillips, "Island on an Island," *New York Times Magazine*, August 21, 1960, p. 26.

promote an incident in order to justify an attack against the regime.[56] Such arguments have not served, of course, to convince the United States that it should abandon the base. But, in fact, Cuba has from the very beginning recognized that it was powerless to evict the United States from Guantánamo either politically, militarily, or legally; as a result, it has taken a consistently moderate approach to this issue of contention with the United States. For example, first in 1960 Cuban President Osvaldo Dorticós stated: "In the proper time and through the proper political procedures we will claim the territory, [but] we would never commit the stupidity of providing the North American Empire with a pretext to invade us by attacking the naval base." [57] Then, in 1964, Castro asserted that the Guantánamo issue was "not urgent," and that force would not be used against the base.[58] Later, in November 1971, he stated with confidence that his country would "eventually" get the U.S. Navy out of Guantánamo, and perhaps "without firing a shot." [59] And, in fact, Cuba has taken no direct action against the base, nor, rather inexplicably, has it made the existence of a foreign base in its territory the focus of a major campaign in international forums such as the United Nations.

The only significant incident involving the Guantánamo base occurred on February 6, 1964 when Castro cut off the base's water supply in retaliation for the U.S. "seizure" of four Cuban fishing vessels. Prior to this date Cuba had supplied the base with two million gallons of water a day, pumped four and one-half miles from the Yateras River, for which it received some $14,000 per month.[60] But, no treaty provision was violated by this action; the supplying of water to the base had been the subject of a separate contractual agreement first signed in 1938. The Navy quickly installed desalinization equipment and has not since used Cuban water. But the incident did result in the tightening of the base's defenses, which in turn led to the dismissal of hundreds of Cubans who had been employed as workers on the base. Thus, at this point the Castro regime had deprived itself of all economic benefits from the base—the $3,386.25 a year it received in rent, the $14,000 per month from the supply of water, and most of the $7.8 million a year the base-employed Cuban workers took into the Cuban economy.[61] Simultaneously, Castro surrounded the base with a permanent ring of Cuban troops; but, even so, State Depart-

---

56. See Kenner and Petras, *Fidel Castro Speaks*, p. 29.
57. *Newsweek*, November 14, 1960, p. 27.
58. *New York Times*, February 20, 1964, p. 1.
59. *The Washington Post*, November 23, 1971, p. A8.
60. *Life*, July 18, 1960, p. 20.
61. *Ibid.*

ment sources indicate that approximately 50-60 Cubans annually manage to escape from Cuba through the base.[62]

From a military standpoint, Guantánamo is directly related to the geopolitics of the Caribbean and the latter's strategic importance to U. S. security, a traditional concern originally centered around the possibility that a hostile power in the area might pose a military threat for the Gulf of Mexico, the mouth of the Mississippi River, and the approaches to the Panama Canal. As such, American military strategists have seen Guantánamo as a vital link in the chain of U. S. Caribbean bases stretching from Cuba to Panama. The popular view of this base and its importance to U. S. security is reflected in this quotation from a national news magazine:

> The base itself is considered by U.S. naval officers to be one of the finest in the world. It covers 45 square miles, has an excellent deep harbor, air strips long enough to handle the fastest jets, and facilities to train and garrison thousands of U.S. sailors and marines, plus civilian workers...In wartime, Guantánamo and the military installations in the Panama Canal can insure U.S. control of the Caribbean Sea area and defend its approaches to the Panama Canal.[63]

Up to and including World War II, the Guantánamo base did play a vital strategic role in the defense of the United States and the Western Hemisphere. This was at the time when one hostile battleship could endanger the Panama Canal. Since then, however, technological advances in modern weaponry and in delivery systems have changed the realities of the geopolitical perspective and, consequently, the strategic value of Guantánamo. Retired Rear Admiral Gene LeRocque— former director of the Inter-American Defense College and now head of the privately-funded Center for Defense Information—has been quoted as saying Guantánamo "no longer serves our strategic interests;" moreover, he called the base a "vestige of U. S. imperialism." [64]

Most discerning observers, as well as the U. S. military itself, then, recognize Guantánamo's minimal strategic value. More than a decade ago *Life Magazine* editorialized:

> With the increasing mobility and endurance of modern armaments, military men concede that Gitmo is no longer absolutely essential to American defense. But, they would hate to lose it.[65]

62. Private interviews with State Department area officials (November, 1971).
63. *U. S. News & World Report*, February 17, 1964, pp. 38-39.
64. *The Times of the Americas*, May 24, 1972, p. 8.
65. *Life*, July 18, 1960, p. 20.

9

The military would "hate to lose it" not so much, then, for the traditional geopolitical and strategic reasons that the base *controls* the Windward Passage from the Atlantic to the Caribbean, *commands* the nexus of maritime traffic through the area, *assures* the safety of the air routes from the east coast of the United States to the west coast of South America, or *guarantees* the security of the approaches to the Panama Canal, but because it continues to be practically *useful* to the U. S. Navy.

Guantánamo is, unquestionably, an excellent naval facility, particularly for training purposes. Its location provides near-perfect weather conditions for both aerial and naval shakedown and refresher training and the necessary isolation for gunnery and anti-submarine warfare practice. In addition, over the years the facility has been excellently equipped to support its now basic mission: namely, that of being an isolated, warm-water training base for the fleet. But, even as a training base, Guantánamo is replaceable; in fact, today the near-by Roosevelt Roads Naval Base in Puerto Rico already duplicates most of Guantánamo's functions—and at less cost. Under present conditions, Guantánamo is exceedingly expensive to maintain and operate. Due to its total isolation from Cuba, tours of duty for most of its 6-8,000 men are cut short, all its water must be desalinated, and its food is brought in from either the United States or Jamaica.

Thus, few thoughtful observers contend that Guantánamo is today militarily indispensable for the United States; many, however, do aver that its strategic importance is directly tied to its continued political importance. Hanson W. Baldwin, the former military editor of the *New York Times*, for example, sees Guantánamo's political implications in this light:

> Gitmo's political and psychological importance transcends its military utility. The base stands today as a symbol of U.S. power and prestige. Its future is clearly linked with the fortune of other U.S. overseas bases—particularly with the future of the Panama Canal Zone and of Chaguaramos, our leased base in Trinidad. What we do in one will affect all. If we are bullied, bluffed, blackmailed, or persuaded to abandon Guantánamo, the effects will be apparent throughout the Caribbean and in Latin America.[66]

But, if it is asserted that negotiations for a possible modified status would jeopardize American "rights" in other comparable situations, then it would seem that the U. S.'s disposition in recent years to satisfy Panamanian desires in terms of the canal should have the effect

66. *New York Times Magazine*, January 10, 1966, p. 112.

of loosening U. S. attitudes regarding the possibility of negotiating with Castro over Guantánamo.[67] And, indeed, although administration officials do not state so publicly, in private interviews many confide that some modification in the status of Guantánamo is probably inevitable. They emphasize, however, that this issue would more likely be taken up after the resolution of several higher priority items and only within the context of the total Cuban settlement question. This subject has been alluded to by Deputy Assistant Secretary of State Robert A. Hurwitch, who has stated publicly:

> ... if we were to have a completely new relationship with the present government or a future government of Cuba, I then think the question of Guantánamo would not be, you know, a major problem.[68]

Although a provision for a U. S. naval station was included in the Platt Amendment of 1901, the actual legal basis for Guantánamo stems from an agreement signed by the two countries in February 1903, which was subsequently amended and reaffirmed in the Treaty of Relations of 1934.[69] The most significant difference between this agreement and the treaty that the United States concluded with Panama during the same historical period is that in the latter the United States was accorded the right of exclusive jurisdiction and control of a specific area in *perpetuity*, whereas the term in the former was left open-ended—that is, until modification or abrogation was decided upon by *both* parties. There is, therefore, no established machinery or procedure for a unilateral change in status. The United States has, of course, no right to occupancy other than that which rests upon the international agreements with Cuba.[70] Therefore, Guantánamo is not

67. For complete documentation on the present status of the Panama Canal and the progress in current negotiations, see U. S. Congress, House of Representatives, Committee on Foreign Affairs, *Panama Canal 1971*, Hearing Before the Sub-Committee on Inter-American Affairs, Washington: Government Printing Office, 1971, and U. S. Congress, House of Representatives, Committee of Foreign Affairs, *Cuba and the Caribbean*, Hearings Before the Sub-Committee on Inter-American Affairs, Washington: Government Printing Office, 1970, pp. 70-88.

68. U. S. Congress, Senate, *Aircraft Hijacking Convention*, Hearings Before the Committee on Foreign Relations, Washington: Government Printing Office, 1971, p. 83.

69. Joseph Lazar, "'Cession in Lease' of the Guantánamo Bay Naval Station and Cuba's 'Ultimate Sovereignty'" *American Journal of International Law*, Vol. 63 (1969), p. 117.

70. This point is disputed by some international lawyers. For example, Joseph Lazar argues that the 1903 and later agreements merely confirmed pre-existing rights over the territory of Guantánamo, rights which the United States

considered part of the United States even for such purposes as marriages and births,[71] and, in further contrast with the Panama case, various restrictions were placed on the use of the base, such as the type of commercial enterprises permitted on the territory.[72]

The Castro regime has used two arguments to support its contention that the United States "illegally" occupies Guantánamo. One is the assertion that, since it did not sign the original agreement and treaty, it is not bound to respect them. Here the Cuban legal argument is weak, for not only did the Castro regime early indicate that it would respect Cuba's international obligations,[73] but also international law is quite clear on this point on the basis of the so-called Doctrine of Succession of Treaty Obligations.[74] Another Cuban legal argument contends that the provisions have no force, inasmuch as the original agreement was imposed upon Cuba under the threat that American military forces would have remained there in 1903 had the Cubans not agreed to sign. This argument is negated by the fact that the agreement was reaffirmed through the treaty of 1934. A more persuasive legal argument (not yet employed by Cuba) is advanced by legal scholar Gary L. Maris,[75] who suggests that Cuba's position can be affirmed by virtue of the rule of *Rebus Sic Stantibus* (the abandonment of treaty obligations because of changed conditions). He asserts that the pertinent agreements were predicated on two fundamental assumptions: mutual friendship and common defense. Therefore, since quite obviously neither of these two conditions obtains today, Cuba can rightfully assert a legitimate legal claim for the unilateral abrogation of the treaty governing the U. S. occupation of Guantánamo.

Despite the legal argumentation surrounding Guantánamo, the

---

had acquired in Cuba under international law through conquest and from the Treaty of Paris (1898) with Spain. The United States government does not, however, officially advance this interpretation.

71. Previously marriages on the base could be sanctioned only under Cuban law. Today personnel cannot be married there, since U. S. law still does not apply for this purpose; they have to go to the States or to Puerto Rico to be married under U. S. law. Citizenship by birth is even more nebulous: children of American parents born on the base, previously and now, are not Cuban through *jus soli* and are Americans only through *jus sanguinis* (see Gary L. Maris, "International Law and Guantánamo," *Journal of Politics*, Vol. 29, No. 2 (May 1967), pp. 261-286).

72. See Gary L. Maris, "The Rights of Occupancy," *American Journal of International Law*, Vol. 63 (1969), pp. 114-116.

73. See *New York Times*, January 30, 1959, p. 7.

74. See Maris, "International Law and Guantánamo," pp. 280-284.

75. *Ibid.*, p. 283.

issue is today, and in all probability will continue to be, fundamentally political. If the United States refuses to discuss the matter, no legal remedy can be obtained. Some Americans are fearful that full abandonment of the base now would make it a gift to the Soviet Union,[76] and almost all policy makers deem it inadvisable to make a modification in the status of Guantánamo one of the first steps toward accommodation. Guantánamo remains, therefore, a latent issue and another of the obstacles to be removed for the full settlement of U. S.-Cuban differences.

The Cuban Exiles: An Analytical Sketch

Without question, Cuba's most successful "export" from the very beginning of the Castro period has not been revolution, but the physical removal of its domestic enemies. For whatever reason individual Cubans came to reject the new order, the decision to part physically from their homeland was made by enough people to develop into probably the greatest mass migration in the history of the Western Hemisphere. Latest estimates provided by the Department of State indicate that approximately 560,000 persons have left Cuba since 1959 to settle in other countries—all but 50,000 in the continental United States or Puerto Rico.[77]

The history of revolution seemingly belies the notion that total societal transformation can take place without large sacrifices of men and property. In most modern revolutions, such as in Mexico, Russia, and China, the destruction of the prior political, economic, and social order seemed to be a necessary concomitant to the achievement of revolutionary goals. On the basis of these models, then, a reasonable conclusion would be that, without violence both preceding and subsequent to the revolutionary victory, there simply would never have been a Mexican, Russian, or Chinese revolution. Cuba, however, appears to be an exception to the general pattern.

Under Castro, Cuban society has been totally transformed; yet, special circumstances have allowed the Cuban revolution to avoid major violence. Even the revolutionary victory was not the product of wide-scale death and destruction. On the contrary, it was more

76. See *Latin American Report*, Vol. 7, No. 7 (1969), p. 2.
77. Figures supplied by the Office of the Cuban Coordinator, Department of State, Washington, D. C. (May, 1972). An independent study conducted in 1972 estimates the Cuban exile population in the United States at 612,648 (see *New York Times*, December 12, 1972, p. 19).

Batista's misuse of counterforce coupled with a generalized antipathy toward Cuba's traditional corrupt political order that produced the demoralization of the regular military forces—the major prop that supported the old system. Once installed, and particularly after Castro decided to radicalize the revolution, the regime still managed to cope with opposition forces without resorting to major violence or excessive coercion. Moreover, neither did Castro have to attract the loyalty of the still largely inchoate opposition through persuasive or co-optative techniques. He had another more convenient alternative, more humane than violence and more sure than persuasion: those who were dissatisfied could simply leave, abandoning their possessions[78] and former life-style to take up residence in other countries. Fundamental to this alternative was, of course, the existence of a convenient and agreeable site toward which the exodus of the disaffected could flow.

Up to the time of the break in diplomatic relations between Cuba and the United States (on January 3, 1961), the Cuban nationals who "permanently" left the island did so rather easily; foreign travel was not restricted, passports were issued, and U. S. visas could be obtained from the still functioning American consulates in Cuba. Once these conditions no longer existed, the movement of Cubans seeking refuge in the United States proceeded in three distinct waves:[79]

Immigration Waves	Number of Refugees Entering the U. S.
I. January 1961 to the Missile Crisis of October 1962	153,534
II. November 1962 to November 1965	29,962
III. December 1965 to March 1972	277,242

Thus, during the period from January 1961 through March 1972, 460,738 Cubans "legally" entered the United States. To this figure, it is necessary to add 11,266 more refugees who arrived "illegally" on boats, rafts, and other make-shift modes of transportation. Another group of 1400 Cubans was taken out of Cuba from February 1968 through May 1971 on special monthly flights from Havana to Matamoros, Mexico, and from there to the United States; these Cubans

78. Many, however, had ample assets already stored overseas. This was the case of most who left in the first migratory wave, mostly *Batistianos*—or close collaborators of the ex-dictator—whose departure might be more aptly described as flight instead of voluntary migration.

79. See *The Times of the Americas*, April 5, 1972, p. 5.

were close relatives of some 800 U.S. citizens on whose behalf the special evacuation flights were arranged.[80] As the above figures also indicate, emigration from Cuba dropped sharply from November 1962 through November 1965. This was due primarily to the limited transportation available for "legal" departures, as well as to obstacles imposed by the Cuban government; some "illegal" escapes were, however, successfully accomplished.

The huge increase in legalized departures, reflected in Wave III, grew out of Castro's announcement on September 28, 1965 that all those who wished to leave the island could do so freely.[81] Immediately thereafter thousands of Cubans rushed to the authorized port of egress (Camarioca, east of Havana) to embark for the United States on any available type of seacraft. To prevent serious accidents and loss of life, as well as to regularize the flow of Cubans out of the island, President Johnson announced that the American people would gladly welcome all these persons into the United States. And, furthermore, through the Swiss (who handle U.S. affairs in Cuba) an agreement was reached with the Castro regime on November 6, 1965,[82] according to which all Cubans registering for emigration would be airlifted out of Cuba at U.S. government expense on twice-daily flights, five days a week. These flights—which cost $ 800 each—[83]evacuated to Miami between 3,000 and 4,000 refugees per month. The registration period for this airlift evacuation ended in May 1966, and most of those who originally registered and desired to leave have now been brought to the United States.

Early in 1972, the Castro government began to interrupt the flow of airlifted refugees for days or weeks at a time, finally stopping the flights altogether. Castro announced that the flights would be permanently suspended, since almost all those registered had already departed. It was possible for him to insist upon this, because technically he had fulfilled the obligations of the original agreement. There are still, however, approximately 94,000 people in Cuba whose relations in the United States have registered them for entry into the

80. U.S. Congress, House of Representatives, Committee on Foreign Affairs, *Cuba and the Caribbean*, Hearings Before the Sub-Committee on Inter-American Affairs, Washington, D.C.: Government Printing Office, 1970, pp. 21 and 160, and information supplied by the Department of State (May 1972). These U.S. citizens and their close relatives were evacuated by the granting of U.S. government repatriation loans covering the transportation expenses. U.S. law requires that these loans be repaid. State Department records show that 800 registered U.S. citizens and 1400 close relatives still remain in Cuba.

81. See *Ibid.*, p. 4.

82. The text of this agreement can be found in *Ibid.*, pp. 5-9.

83. U.S. Congress, *Aircraft Hijacking Convention*, pp. 37 and 39.

country. The U. S. government has approved this additional list, but there has been no corresponding acknowledgment on the part of the Castro regime.[84] Nonetheless, in December 1972, Castro permitted a partial resumption of the "freedom flights" for 3,400 persons.[85] Most of these were elderly or infirm.

The reasons for Castro's refusal to permit the regular continuation of the airlift evacuation flights are not known. However, some State Department officials conjecture that, with most of the potential opposition already out of Cuba, those who have indicated a desire to leave represent no serious disruptive force, and can be advantageously employed in supplementing Cuba's manpower shortage. Throughout the airlift period, the U. S. government justified its continuance on humanitarian principles and as a supplement to the underlying objectives of its anti-Castro isolation policy, which sought to preserve the hope of an active resistance of the Cuban people to the existing regime. In 1970, Deputy Assistant Secretary of State Robert A. Hurwitch defended the airlift with these words:

> Experience has indicated that as long as hope for escape to freedom exists, people living under oppression resist committing themselves to the regime's goals...The refugee airlift, a route to freedom, forestalls the certainty of accommodation to communism of the Cuban people.[86]

In part because of the modified attitude of the U. S. government with respect to the temporary nature of the Castro regime, and in part because of a growing congressional resistance to the continued funding of the entire Cuban refugee program, the United States has not been entirely unhappy about the cessation of the Cuban airlift. The congressional resistance has manifested itself in a concern over the relatively high costs of maintaining not only the airlift itself —which is paid by the Department of State—but the Cuban Refugee Program of the Department of Health, Education, and Welfare. From 1961 through June 1972, this program cost the U. S. government approximately $727 million,[87] of which $144 million was allocated for fiscal year 1972. In addition, voices have been raised about the number of Cubans on welfare rolls, and in a period of scarce employment, there have been complaints that the employed Cubans are "taking"

84. The above information was supplied by the Office of the Cuban Coordinator, Department of State, Washington, D. C. (May, 1972).
85. *New York Times*, December 1, 1972, p. 6.
86. U. S. Congress, *Cuba and the Caribbean*, p. 5.
87. *The Washington Post*, September 1, 1971, p. A12.

jobs from native Americans. The Cuban airlift has also played havoc with the immigration program for the Western Hemisphere, since every Cuban who enters via the airlift route is charged against the hemisphere-wide annual immigration quota of 120,000 when the refugee desires to regularize his immigration status in the United States. As a result, while Cubans enter freely, other prospective Latin American immigrants must wait up to 16 months after meeting all entry requirements, and after their applications have been processed.

Statistics on the composition of the thousands of Cubans in the United States have, by now, indicated trends which have not changed significantly over the past few years:[88]

Cuban Refugees in the United States

By Occupation	Percentage
Children, students, and housewives	64.0
Professional, semi-professional and managerial	6.5
Skilled workers	9.3
Clerical and sales	11.7
Semi-skilled	3.6
Farming and fishing	1.8
Service workers	3.1
	100.0

By Ages	
1 - 18	34.0
19 - 49	44.0
50 - 59	10.5
60 - 65	4.1
66 - above	7.4
	100.0

These figures seem to substantiate, in part, the findings of Richard Fagen and his associates, whose study on Cuban exiles—although based primarily on those Cubans who arrived in the earlier refugee waves—produced this conclusion:

88. These statistics are based on information covering the years up to and including 1969, and are taken from U. S. Congress, *Cuba and the Carribbean*, p. 12. The figures for 1970 remained practically the same in each category (see *The Washington Post*, September 1, 1971, p. A12).

The great preponderance of the refugees are drawn from the wealthier, the better educated, the more urban, and the higher occupational sectors.[89]

By far the greatest concentration of Cuban exiles in the United States is found in the greater Miami area of Florida. The 350,000 Cubans there make Miami the second largest "Cuban" city, fewer than Havana's 1.7 million, but more than Santiago de Cuba (276,000).[90] The exiles of Miami represent an important economic force; there are many Cuban-owned businesses, an all-Spanish television station, three Spanish-speaking radio stations, one daily newspaper, and at least a dozen weekly and bi-weekly Cuban publications. The Cuban exile community in Puerto Rico has also become economically significant.

Politically, disunity continues to be the distinguishing characteristic of the Cuban exile "community" in the United States. Over-all, the exiles have a decided anti-Castro orientation which, in certain areas, must be taken into account politically. This is particularly the case in the Miami area, whose U. S. Congressman Dante B. Fascell is, significantly, Chairman of the House Foreign Affairs Committee's sub-committee on Inter-American affairs. But the political strength of the Cuban exile community even on the anti-Castro question is diluted by the fact that there is still no generally recognized leader or group of leaders around whom a cohesive, anti-Castro movement can be organized. In the early 1960's, there were about 200 anti-Castro exile organizations, but today this interest has waned, and their number has been reduced to perhaps a dozen. Nonetheless, the anti-Castro sentiment is still pervasive enough: immediately before President Nixon's visit to the Soviet Union in May 1972, some 5,000 exiles marched in Washington to protest the alleged prospect that the President might negotiate certain aspects of the Cuban problem with the Soviet Union.[91]

Certain exile groups also continue to stage sporadic running raids against Cuba, one of which occurred on October 12, 1971 against the small Cuban port town of Boca de Sama. It was purportedly carried out by the so-called "Cuban Forces of Liberation" led by 68-year-old José Elías de la Torriente. Castro retaliated by capturing two ships in international waters operated by Cuban exiles; he claimed that they were spying for the CIA.[92] A mini-crisis developed over this inci-

89. Richard Fagen, Richard A. Brody, and Thomas O'Leary, *Cubans in Exile: Disaffection and the Revolution* (Palo Alto: Stanford University Press, 1968), p. 23.
90. *New York Times*, April 18, 1971, p. 26.
91. *The Washington Post*, May 21, 1972, p. D1.
92. *The Washington Post*, December 29, 1971, p. F11.

dent, during which both Cuba and the United States put their military forces on alert. Over-all, however, such exile activity has diminished considerably. And the U. S. government has insisted that it be stopped entirely. Following the above incident, the government issued a formal warning:

> The U. S. government warned Cuban exile leaders in Miami that they would be prosecuted to the fullest extent of the law if they engage in anti-Castro activity from U. S. soil.[93]

The massive departure from Cuba of the socially and economically better situated elements of Cuban society, besides removing the most immediate source of potential opposition, also contributed greatly to solidifying the support of those who enthusiastically embraced the new order—the rural masses, the majority of the youth, and the new bureaucrats, party leaders, and managerial élites.[94] By replacing the departed exiles, these groups gained a new dignity, social mobility, and the opportunity to take part actively in the prosecution of the revolution's goals. To generalize, it might be said that the refugees share the Cuban hope of a fully sovereign and independent Cuba, but object to what they view as the "evils" of the present regime—Castro's "totalitarianism," the close association with "international communism" and, for many, the nature of Cuba's heavily socialized economic system. In other words, even in the absence of "Castroism," they would still want to reaffirm the programs and ideals advocated during the initial phase of the present revolution, such as "positive" agrarian reform, the democratization of urban and rural labor unions, a protected domestic industry, and full adherence to other points specified in the liberal 1940 constitution.[95] In short, they too want *revolution* for Cuba, but differ as to what variant of this concept should be employed. This, of course, constitutes the very crux of the exiles' original alienation from the revolutionary process pursued by the Castro regime.

In the exile demonstration referred to previously, Washington coordinator José Antonio Font called not only for the "absolute independence" and the "political and economic sovereignty" of Cuba, but also insisted that "Cuba must be free and Cubans must free her." [96] That the impulse for Cuban "freedom" can come from the exiles

93. *The Washington Post*, January 29, 1972, p. A9.
94. Fagen, *et al.*, *Cubans in Exile*, p. 119.
95. See, for example, Javier Felipe Pazos Vea, "Cuba—Long Live the Revolution!," *New Republic* (November 3, 1962), pp. 15-19.
96. *The Washington Post*, May 21, 1972, p. D1.

remains, however, a moot point. As early as 1962, thoughtful Cubans had already recognized that the role of the exiles in the determination of Cuba's future political development could, at best, be peripheral:

> The exiles can help in various ways, but it is up to those who remain in Cuba to determine the strategy to be followed.[97]

Thus far the desired internal opposition to the Castro regime has not developed, and most probably none will, so long as the attacks against the regime are viewed by the Cubans in Cuba as threats to the *revolution* itself—which they see might be endangered if "Castroism" is eliminated.[98] And, given the counter-revolutionary nature of the earlier direct attacks against the Castro regime, led by right-wing elements and/or the United States, such fears have a basis in fact. But, if the present regime should be overturned, what would be the more likely role of the Cuban exiles? Deep down, the exiles must know, but most will never openly express or admit, that they will probably never play a decisive role in the future development of Cuba if and when Castro leaves the scene. This task more properly belongs to those who served and shared in the trials, the anguish, and, at times, the successes of the Cuban people's experiment in the construction of a new society.

---

97. Raúl Chibás, "What Next for Cuba?—An Exile's View," *New Republic* (November 10, 1962), p. 9.

98. Javier Felipe Pazos Vea, *New Republic*, p. 18.

CHAPTER IX

THE POLICY ALTERNATIVES:
A COST-BENEFIT ANALYSIS

In the broadest strategic sense, there are but two policy alternatives for any nation whose vital interests are engaged in a given international problem: the nation can contemplate negotiation or warfare. The option selected by the United States against the Cuban revolutionary regime has been fundamentally that of warfare, defined as a belligerent hostility. Although conditioned to an important degree by Cuba's words and actions, the hostility has remained steady through three policy stages. These stages, which are differentiated by the goals sought in each sequence, encompass the entire period during which the containment policy framework was first built and then elaborated. Today the policy continues. These stages are:

Stage	Ultimate Goals Pursued
I. 1960-1963	Overthrow of the Castro regime and the return to the *status quo ante*, with modifications.
II. 1964-1968	Emergence of a new, more reasonable government in Cuba.
III. 1969-1975	Ambiguous.

The ultimate end toward which U. S. Cuban policy is directed today cannot be easily discerned. On the one hand, the basic containment policy framework of political isolation and economic denial continues to be tenaciously advocated and supported; yet, on the other hand, most of the attitudes, specific objections, and hopeful expectations upon which the policy was constructed are now no longer considered appropriate, pertinent, or attainable. Nonetheless, officially, the same policy orientation is pursued on the basis of a U. S. concern for (1) Cuba's vociferous hostility toward the United States, (2) Cuban "interventionist behavior" and (3) Castro's policy of "seeking ever closer" military ties with the Soviet Union.[1] The United States emphasized these very same points during Stage II (1964-1968), but the abolition of such practices was not considered the ultimate goal pursued by the prosecution of the hemispheric-wide, anti-Castro "containment" policy. Neither was the direct elimination of Castro. The expectation was, rather, that the elaborate set of supportive policy actions, if firmly maintained, would so discredit and weaken the regime that a new government would eventually arise in Cuba with which the United States could more easily come to some basic understanding. And, in the meantime, the supportive action lines of the policy were intended to keep such disruptive influences as the "export of revolution" to a minimum. The assumption was, in short, that the problems associated with the Castro regime would disappear along with the regime. This viewpoint was similarly reflected in the academically-oriented literature. In an essay directed toward the elucidation of future prospects for U. S.-Cuban relations, Bayless Manning stated, in effect, that only time would provide a solution to the U. S.'s Cuban problem in the form of a successor government—but only, he emphasized, if the United States stood firm in its present policy. Specifically his prognosis was:

> One suspects that Castro will either be inspired to do something foolish that will lead to his violent destruction or will find himself forced to renegotiate his way back into the Western Hemisphere at a considerable price.[2]

1. See U. S. Congress, Senate, *United States Policy Towards Cuba*, Hearing Before the Senate Foreign Relations Committee, Washington: Government Printing Office, 1971, p. 7, and Secretary of State William Rogers' statements at the April, 1972 OAS Assembly meeting in Washington, D. C. (*The Department of State Newsletter*, No. 133 [May 1972], pp. 14-17).
2. Bayless Manning, "An Overall Perspective," in John Plank, ed., *Cuba and the United States: Long-Range Perspectives* (Washington: The Brookings Institution, 1967, p. 237.)

If, however, the early removal of the Castro regime is no longer viewed as attainable, nor particularly essential for U. S. interests (the current official attitude), the justificatory keystone upon which the policy framework rests is effectively dislodged.

U. S. Cuban policy today consists, therefore, of a policy framework designed to achieve goals now no longer sought. Furthermore, the effectiveness of continued reliance on this policy framework is questionable even in terms of medium-range objectives. It can be argued, for example, that the policy can and does have a decided effect on Cuban instigation of insurgency in the hemisphere, but neither Cuban support for revolution, its military ties with the Soviet Union, nor its hostility toward the United States can be advantageously modified in favor of U. S. interests by the continued pursuit of the dual policies of political isolation and economic denial. On the contrary, the policy encourages the intensification rather than the moderation of the Cuban impulse to persist in such undertakings. Present U. S. Cuban policy, instead of being a design for the pursuit of a defined set of ultimate goals, has become primarily an instrument with which to inflict revenge upon Cuba as an example to others who might still be inspired by Cuban revolutionary ideals.

Specifically, then, the continuation of the containment policy framework serves not to further progress toward attaining defined *goals*, but to articulate and defend a set of retaliatory *principles*—notably, (1) to punish Cuba for its anti-U. S. belligerency and (2) to denigrate the Cuban example in the eyes of the world. Neither is a particularly edifying basis for the foreign policy of a country deeply committed to the development of peaceful and constructive relationships with all nations. Another even more petty purpose behind the maintenance of the ongoing policy is the apparent conviction that any U. S. move toward accommodation would enhance Castro's prestige and "lend him the stature of the international scene he seeks but does not enjoy." [3] Thus, America's continuing disdain and distrust of Castro translate into support for a policy that attempts to tarnish the image of Castro's revolutionary leadership and his place in history.

U. S. Cuban policy today has become somewhat incoherent in the sense that general policy lines continue to be followed in the absence of a clear conception of what precise ends are beings pursued. This suggests, therefore, that the over-all policy is in a period of transition, and quite possibly nearing a point of transformation. Although the U. S. policy of rigid opposition to the Castro regime remains seem-

3. U. S. Congress, *United States Policy Towards Cuba*, p. 7.

ingly unchanged, the only fundamental complaint the U. S. makes against Cuba today centers around the latter's continued *support* for the export of revolution. This is a substantial change from the former policy line which viewed all of Cuba's connections with the Soviet Union as likewise non-negotiable elements in the Cuban-U. S. adversary relationship.[4] But does this mean that the cessation of Cuban support for hemispheric insurgency has now been elevated to the position of being the primary or ultimate goal of U. S. Cuban policy? At no point has the term "export of revolution" been adequately defined; hence, despite the almost total absence of *active* Cuban support in the export of subversion, the United States continues to base its entire anti-Castro policy on its supposed existence—and the risks for the Americas should the containment policy framework be dismantled. If stopping the export of revolution were the principal goal of U. S. Cuban policy, it could be attained by devising a way of insuring that Cuba would continue doing what it is not doing today. A logical way to encourage this development would be to tie the lifting of sanctions to a specific definition of what constitutes an unacceptable level of such activity. That this or some similar type of measure has not been implemented supports the thesis that the complaint against Cuba's "export of revolution" serves more as a facade behind which are hidden other policy purposes more fundamental to the central thrust of today's U. S. Cuban policy.

The basic alternatives, or policy strategies, available to U. S. policy makers for dealing with Cuba are limited. Senator J. William Fulbright saw only three possible options in 1964:

> There are and have been three options open to the United States with respect to Cuba: first, the removal of the Castro regime by invading and occupying the island; second, an effort to weaken and ultimately bring down the regime by a policy of political and economic boycott, and, finally, acceptance of the Castro regime as a disagreeable reality and annoyance, but one which is not likely to be removed in the near future because of the unavailability of acceptable means of removing it.[5]

Senator Fulbright's listing is, however, incomplete. The range of possible alternatives that were—and are—*theoretically* available to U. S. policy makers can be expanded. The employment of any given policy

4. George Ball, "Principles of Our Policy Toward Cuba," *Department of State Bulletin* (May 1, 1964), p. 739.
5. J. William Fulbright, "Foreign Policy: Old Myths and New Realities," *Vital Speeches* (April 15, 1964), p. 38.

strategy depends upon how a time and circumstantial framework is interpreted; and this interpretation, in itself, is highly conditioned by such factors as preferences, attitudes, constituency pressures, and the impact of operational structures that process the assessment of pertinent variables.

Possible Lines of U. S. Strategy: Cuba

(a) *Direct Military Action.* This alternative was employed at the time of the Bay of Pigs invasion in 1961—albeit not fully, since only exiles and not U. S. troops were directly deployed, and, in the end, only limited U. S. logistic and air support was provided to the invading force. Owing to probable unfavorable domestic and international political repercussions and the possibility of engendering a situation of confrontation with the Soviet Union, this option has not been seriously considered since the missile crisis of 1962. On the latter occasion, former Secretary of Defense McNamara estimated that an invading force of U. S. troops would have had to expect 40-50,000 casualties.[6] Today the far better equipped and trained Cuban forces would be even more effective in their attempts to repulse an invasion of a conventional type.

(b) *Enforced Blockade.* In accordance with generally recognized precepts of international law, a complete blockade of Cuba would constitute an act of warfare. As such, this option would most probably be resorted to only under the most dire circumstances. Again, its employment would carry the great risk of engaging the Soviet Union in a direct confrontation.

(c) *High-Intensity Containment* (Further Economic Sanctions). Although highly improbable at this point in time the United States and the members of the OAS could harden their opposition by adding to the political and economic measures already taken against the Castro regime. Here one's imagination can run wild, for the possibilities are endless. For example, they might refuse to trade with any country trading with Cuba, they might advocate a complete break with the Soviet Union until the latter breaks off its relationship with the revolutionary regime, or they could even refuse to attend —or pay dues to—the United Nations until Cuba was branded an aggressor and/or expelled from the organization. Another possible

6. See Arthur Schlesinger, Jr., *A Thousand Days: JFK in the White House* (Boston: Houghton Miffling Co., 1965), p. 851.

10

measure, once advocated by Richard Nixon, could be the closing down of internal markets to any foreign company that did business with Cuba.[7] The practicality and effectiveness of implementing any additional sanction are, of course, factors which would have to be taken into account.

(d) *Moderate-Intensity Containment.* This alternative corresponds to the type of political isolation and economic denial policies which have become the framework for today's anti-Castro containment policy posture. The "moderate-intensity" qualifier refers to the relative degree of pressure the containment policy intends to exert upon the Castro regime.

(e) *Low-Intensity Containment.* This strategy line depicts current U. S. policy toward Cuba. It should be viewed as a posture assumed during the transitional stage between the full maintenance of the containment policy framework and the adoption of more conciliatory and accommodative attitudes on key policy questions. In a concrete sense, this means that where before there was concern and rage, today something between indifference and a recognition of realities exists. In the meantime, however, the containment policy framework remains operational and no direct move toward accommodation takes place.

(f) *Regularization of Relations.* This strategy contemplates the situation of a gradualist approach toward accommodation. The steps taken and measures adopted would be minimal, but decisive in terms of developing the basis for a firm and lasting rapprochement with Cuba. Small-scale diplomatic and commercial relations would be restored, although no significant trade, for example, would take place until, through negotiations, settlement could be reached on such obstacles as the questions of claims, sugar sales, and the status of Guantánamo. The objective of this strategy line is clearly to open the door to dialogue on the basis of a self-respecting recognition of mutual interests.

(g) *Normalization of Relations.* This strategy line assumes the existence—varying in each context—of "normal" diplomatic and political relationships: there would be full diplomatic and commercial representation; trade exchanges would take place; credits could be advanced; and America's technical and economic aid might be forthcoming. The alternative is a possibility even with a continued Soviet presence in Cuba; it would most probably become U. S. policy if Castro or a successor government decided—and had the power and maneuverability—to return fully to the American fold.

7. See the reference to this proposal in *Vital Speeches* (April 15, 1964), p. 39.

It is now possible to see that Senator Fulbright's third option—"acceptance of the Castro regime as a disagreeable reality and annoyance"—does not necessarily represent the advocacy of accommodation with the Castro regime. It seems, on the contrary, more like the current policy. Today the United States appears to be resigned to the idea that a Castro-type regime is more likely than unlikely to remain a long-range feature of the Cuban political scene; nevertheless, it seemingly places a low priority on any attempt to change the present low-keyed adversary relationship—particularly in view of Cuba's apparent refusal to reciprocate a more friendly attitude. For now, the seemingly placid seas of policy drift appear preferable to the possibilities of being dragged into the maelstrom of complicating issues surrounding any decisive move toward rapprochement with Cuba. Nonetheless, the thrust of this policy takes it closer to a forward position of modest accommodation than a fall-back to a more rigid, oppositionalist policy orientation.

Unless, then, some wholly unexpected development emerges to change radically present discernible attitudinal and contextual trends, it appears that the only alternatives open to U.S. policy makers in terms of Cuba are either (1) the continuation of the current "low-intensity" containment policy strategy or (2) the adoption of an accommodative policy strategy whose goal would be to seek actively—but prudently and gradually—an *eventual* "regularization" of relations with the Castro regime. The probable consequences for the United States of changing to the new strategy will be traced below. Before this can be done, however, it is necessary to weigh the implications of probable Cuban futures from the standpoint of the Soviet Union and of Castro.

At present or in the future, the Soviet Union has essentially only three alternatives with respect to its relationship with Cuba: it can (1) withdraw (2) maintain the present relationship or (3) take steps to make the relationship even more intimate. It should be noted that in the past four years the two countries have, by mutual agreement, established their closest association of the Cuban revolutionary period. Castro has encouraged this trend as a means of obtaining increased sums of vital developmental assistance. The Soviet leadership has also sought to develop closer ties in an effort to make Russian economic and technical aid to Cuba more effective. For better or worse, the Soviet Union must continue to support its Cuban ally; and since it cannot, for political and ideological reasons, afford to allow the revolution to fail economically, it becomes advantageous for the Soviets to contribute somewhat more and to become more involved in order to make the Cuban economy strong and self-sustaining. From

131

the Soviet standpoint, the endeavor, if successful, would also effectively counter the U. S. denigration of the Cuban example as a developmental model for the Third World.

In any event, it seems reasonable to assume that increased Soviet involvement in Cuba has enhanced the possibilities for greater Soviet influence and leverage. Thus, the assumption long held by many U. S. observers that the unseating of Castro will inevitably produce domestic chaos in Cuba [8] can no longer go unchallenged; an intensive and prolonged Soviet involvement there could well mean that, upon Castro's fall or death, not chaos but a strengthening of the effective power of the already structured—although now impotent—Communist Party could result. And, if so, almost assuredly such a development would signify a constricted degree of Cuban independence vis-à-vis the Soviet Union, a prospect the United States may wish to discourage—unless, of course, it has no objection to a *heavy*, long-term Soviet presence in Cuba.

Castro, on the other hand, has long recognized that his personal power and authority—as well as Cuba's independence—depend largely upon the possibilities open to him for autonomous action. This Castro has continually sought; and with great virtuosity he has achieved the necessary degree of maneuverability by combining his own unmatched power base with a talent for modifying Cuban support on given ideological, tactical, and party issues to suit Cuban interests. The risk for Castro in the growing Cuban-Soviet intimacy is, then, the possibility of seeing his area of maneuverability narrowed. For the moment, since economic success has become the center of his concerns—both for the revolution and for his image and reputation as a Third World, rather than strictly revolutionary, leader—the increased Soviet assistance is essential. But, despite the current trend, it is not beyond the realm of the possible that Castro may well shortly see minimal accommodation with the United States as the only option open to him for expanding his leverage with the Soviets. This could also enhance his reputation as a "nation builder" identified more closely with the Third World. Whatever qualms the United States might have about contributing to the respectability of the Castro image would have to be assessed against the background of risks involved in waiting to deal with some other person or government in Cuba. Castro is, after all, probably the only one who could conceivably come to some agreement with the United States without seeming to betray the Cuban people's revolution.

What follows, then, is not necessarily the advocacy of a strategy

8. See, for example, Bayless Manning, "An Overall Perspective," p. 238.

preference, but an enumeration of *some* of the more probable and pertinent consequences that *might* result from the adoption of the type of accommodative orientation most likely under prevailing conditions, as well as the more common arguments in rebuttal to the points raised:

U. S. Cuban Policy

Alternative Future Balance Sheet

Decision Contemplated: Should the United States adopt an accommodative policy strategy whose goal would be to seek actively—but with prudence and gradually—an eventual "regularization" of relations with the Castro regime, assuming that a positive Castro response would be forthcoming?

The Probable Consequences

Pro	Con
(1) The two countries can begin a process of converting a hostile, adversary relationship into one which seeks mutually - beneficial cooperation.	(1) The effort at détente will convey the impression that the United States lacks the resolve to deal firmly with countries whose actions harm fundamental American interests, and may well encourage similar actions on the part of other governments and/ or movements.
(2) Direct talks are more likely to produce tangible results than no contact or indirect communication through third parties.	(2) The official contact alone will legitimize the revolutionary regime, adding to its stability and consolidation while, simultaneously, enhancing the respectability of Castro both as a revolutionary and a nation builder.
(3) Permanent diplomatic and commercial representation might be agreed to.	(3) Permanent official ties offer no guarantee of favorable results on questions affecting U. S. inte-

133

rests, and, domestically, this would bring cries of betrayal from the Cuban exile community, as well as expressions of concern from powerful economic groups.

(4) Chances are increased that initial steps can be taken toward resolving such pending issues as the export of revolution, the entire set of sanctions against Cuba, Guantánamo, exile attacks against Cuba, excessive stocks of Soviet arms in Cuba, sugar sales, aerial survelliance flights over Cuba, claims of U. S. citizens, trade, refugees, exchanges of people and information programs, travel, etc.

(4) Unless full normalization of relations can be achieved, most of these potentially disturbing issues are better left untouched.

(5) It provides Castro with the *opportunity* to lessen Cuban political and economic dependence upon the Soviet Union.

(5) Strategically, the Soviet Union will still be able to use Cuba for its purposes—particularly its naval and subversive purposes.

(6) It is likely that *any* U. S.-Cuban rapprochement will diminish to some degree Soviet influence in Cuba.

(6) The Soviet presence will remain in Cuba.

(7) Negotiations with Castro may well be preferable to the uncertainty of dealing with an unknown successor or government.

(7) Any future government in Cuba could be no worse than the Castro regime.

(8) Chances are increased for Cuban participation in regional economic and political programs or institutions—probably not the OAS, but perhaps programs involving unified Caribbean relationships.

(8) Hemispheric harmony will not be restored; in fact, it is likely that the inter-American system would be permanently damaged, inasmuch as Cuba would remain outside of and work against the OAS as presently constituted.

134

(9) Any amount of U. S. - Cuban trade will begin the process of redirecting Cuba's present artificial commercial patterns away from the communist party-states and toward its traditional partners. U. S. replacement parts, if traded, will help preserve the Cuban market for future U. S. sales.	(9) Any U. S. - Cuban trade will strengthen Cuba's prospects for creating a viable economy, which, if achieved, will symbolically prove the applicability of the Cuban socialist, anti-U. S. approach to economic development.
(10) The initial contact with Castro and his regime will underscore, and provide true symmetry to, the administration's declared readiness to deal with governments "as they are."	(10) Cuban belligerency toward the U. S. and its export of revolution may well continue.
(11) The basic move toward accommodation is undertaken prior to and without the political embarrassment of a possible OAS vote overturning U. S. objections to a change in hemispheric policy toward Cuba.	(11) The Latin American countries do not want a modified relationship with Castro's Cuba, and will agree to such only if strongly urged by the United States.

Because there is no way of knowing precisely what might occur should even minimal conciliation between the United States and Cuba take place, the arguments on both sides can appear equally persuasive. Nonetheless, this analysis has attempted to demonstrate that, whatever the arguments, there has been a gradual progression in U. S. Cuban policy in recent years, in the sense of a loosening of American objections on several key points. But, despite the heightened degree of realism, the path along which the policy has advanced continues to be obstructed by (1) the difficulty in breaking through the accumulated effects of the mutual hostility pattern, and (2) the highly charged atmosphere which still surrounds any discussion of the Cuban issue.

Moreover, there is every indication that U. S. policy makers are simply not interested today in grappling with the problems that would be involved in a fundamentally modified relationship with Cuba. Similarly, Castro seems equally content to let things remain, for the moment, as they are. In the meantime, the principal objection to persisting in the present policy line toward Cuba will continue to be that it provides no flexibility for dealing with the long-range implications and consequences of the Cuban revolution and the Castro regime in terms of broader American foreign policy interests. Even a minimal breakthrough in communications would tend to expand the radius of maneuverability. There is also the consideration that the present policy strategy is actually counter-productive, stimulating rather than discouraging the very Cuban behaviors which the U. S. finds most objectionable—Castro's brutish anti-American oratory, Cuba's close ties with the Soviet Union, and Cuban support for revolution in Latin America. It furthermore assures that Soviet influence in Cuba and Latin America will, at a minimum, continue at present levels, and gives the Russians further incentive to continue using Cuba for strategic maritime purposes.

Ideally, the United States could institute a series of low-cost initiatives that, while not inviting a specific rebuff, would represent a clear signal to its Cuban adversary of a positive interest in modifying the present relationship. The difficulty here resides in the fact that, since the anti-Cuban containment policy has been constructed over a multi-lateral foundation (the formal inter-American system), opportunities for discreet, unilateral moves are severely reduced. Almost any measure the United States might contemplate—for example, a partial lifting of the economic embargo—could not be done without either directly infringing an OAS commitment or instigating a long prior debate in the OAS on the merits of the entire Cuban issue.

Whatever the arguments marshalled in support of a basic modification in U. S. Cuban policy, the United States has decided not to engage now in any endeavor conducive to arranging a fundamentally changed relationship with the Cuban revolutionary regime. It is therefore futile to expect that U. S. Cuban policy can be, at present, anything other than what it is. That the policy will soon change—and if so toward the direction of mutual accommodation—although strongly indicated, is still uncertain. Mexico, Canada, and Jamaica in this hemisphere never completely cut their diplomatic or consular ties with Cuba; and during 1972 actual diplomatic exchanges with Chile and Peru presaged the decisions of Argentina, Guyana, Barbados, Trinidad-Tobago (in 1973), Panama (1974), and Venezuela (1975) to establish official relations with Socialist Cuba—all despite the still operative OAS anti-Cuban sanctions. Others will undoubtedly follow. In this light, it seems that an American policy change will inevitably take place—and perhaps sooner than now commonly anticipated.

CHAPTER  X

EPILOGUE

The reelection of Richard Nixon as President of the United States in 1972—along with the retention of Henry Kissinger as his principal adviser on foreign affairs (now also Secretary of State)—assured the unencumbered development of a decidedly distinctive foreign policy style and set of priorities. Despite, or perhaps because of, that administration's efforts to improve relations with such communist countries as the Soviet Union, China, and North Vietnam, no serious movement toward the easing of a fundamentally intransigent anti-Cuban posture took place. Yet, speculation regarding some imminent reassessment and reversal in U. S. Cuban policy continued to persist. This was fed by the suspicion that the détente with other communist states might presage a modified attitude toward Cuba, and the wide-spread belief that Cuba's willingness to negotiate the hijacking issue could represent the initial peg on which an eventual over-all settlement plan might be hung.

Indeed, after weeks of remarkably business-like negotiations conducted through the Swiss, the United States and Cuba concluded an agreement on sky piracy in mid-February 1973,[1] which, thus far, has largely put an end to criminal and deranged skyjackers using Cuba as a convenient haven. It has apparently failed, however, to generate anything beyond its narrow substantive context. Former

1. For the complete text of this agreement, see *New York Times*, February 16, 1973, p. 4.

Secretary of State Rogers was careful to stress that the agreement "does not foreshadow a change of policies as far as the United States is concerned with Cuba."[2] This, of course, reflected a continuation of the consistent hard-line Nixon attitude: that Cuba would have to change its practices and policies toward the United States first. To this, Castro similarly adopted a stiff outward posture: "And what do we care about any change? What do we care what Mr. Nixon may think with his ultra-reactionary and fascist mind?"[3]

Publicly, then, the hijacking negotiations seemingly failed to set the stage for a more rational, unemotional discussion of mutual interests between the two countries. Yet, other developments have taken place in the American domestic, Cuban, exile, and hemispheric environments which point to an erosion in existing policy stances.

The American Domestic Environment

For some time influential political figures like Senator Edward Kennedy have urged a thorough review of U. S. Cuban policy. But now, particularly in light of President Nixon's initiatives in seeking cooperation and the reduction of tensions with former antagonists, others have joined a growing chorus of those who view the present policy as an "anachronism," "counterproductive," and evidence of a "double standard" of diplomatic conduct. The sources of this new encouragement for change are highly significant. Conservative Senator Robert C. Byrd of West Virginia, for one, has publicly urged his congressional colleagues to decide for themselves at what point a harsh, hard-line policy toward Cuba becomes no longer viable, and stated that their answers to this should be guided by "enlightened self-interest."[4] Similarly, Wyoming Senator Gale W. McGee has said that "the time has come for the United States...[to] initiate serious efforts toward the restoration of political and economic relations with Cuba."[5] Furthermore, a group of twelve Republican congressmen issued a report entitled "A Détente With Cuba" in which they call for immediate congressional and presidential consideration of the reestablishment of normal relations between the United States and Cuba, inasmuch as "the time is ripe for diplomatic and economic initiatives to be made."[6]

2. *Ibid.*, p. 5.
3. *San Juan Star*, December 15, 1972, p. 14.
4. *Congressional Record*, March 12, 1973, p. S4335.
5. *Congressional Record*, March 26, 1973, p. S3279.
6. *Congressional Record*, February 20, 1973, p. S2870, and *New York Times*, January 30, 1973, p. 14.

The heightened congressional interest in U. S. Cuban policy, when combined with critical media comment,[7] convincing academic analysis,[8] and other open public debate,[9] all point toward the development of an incipient consensus on the part of concerned publics which cannot help but persuade presidential leadership that a major policy innovation can be acceptably contemplated. With the supportive political environment rapidly coalescing, this process is well on its way. Moreover, the Nixon administration even decided to make an "exception" and allowed three American-owned motor vehicle companies in Argentina and a U. S. locomotive manufacturing concern in Canada to sell specific amounts of their products to the Castro government.[10] Thus, as with China before, those who closely follow U. S. foreign policy concerns perceive that a change in the nation's Cuban policy is now only a matter of time. It requires only the President's willingness and sense of timing in moving toward the adoption of the new policy departure.

The Cuban Environment

Despite Castro's apparent intractability, journalist Herbert L. Matthews reminds us that, "Fidel Castro is nothing if not pragmatic, and he is never afraid to change his tactics."[11] In January 1973 Castro signed a new series of agreements with the Soviet Union [12] which, when added to Cuba's affiliation with COMECON, more than ever indicate the island's growing incorporation into the official communist economic orbit. Nonetheless, few are yet prepared to assert that the Cuban leader has become a mere Soviet puppet.

7. The *Washington Post* and the *New York Times,* for example, have long urged a reassessment of U. S. Cuban policy. For an example of their perspective, see *New York Times,* January 29, 1973, p. 26.

8. A good example is, Edward González, "The United States and Castro: Breaking the Deadlock," *Foreign Affairs,* 50 (July 1972), pp. 722-737.

9. See, for example, *Congressional Conference on U. S.-Cuban Relations,* New Senate Office Building, April 19-20, 1972 (mimeo) and the report of the privately financed Commission on United States-Latin American Relations. (*New York Times,* November 30, 1974, p. 3.)

10. *New York Times,* April 19, 1974, p. 1.

11. *New York Times,* December 14, 1972, p. 47.

12. It was reported that the Soviets agreed to postpone Cuba's $3.5 billion debt repayment schedule until 1986, with no additional interest, and to "pay" Cuba eleven cents (up from six) per pound for its sugar exports to the U. S. S. R. during the period 1973-1980. (See *San Juan Star,* January 10, 1973, p. 10.) This would be in addition to $300 million of other technical and economic aid. The press estimates that there are 1500 Russian civilian technicians presently in Cuba.

Matthews has quoted Castro as saying to him in September 1972: "We will be friendly with those countries who want to be friendly with us, whatever their form of government."[13] Although not sanguine about its applicability to the United States, given prevailing circumstances at that time, Castro clearly included the U. S. in this reference. Moreover, in the wake of the productive hijacking negotiations, his assessment of U. S.-Cuban relations may have also changed. In a radio broadcast, Cuban political commentator Guido García Inclán (whose reporting is recognized as reflecting official government attitudes) cautiously invited the United States to make further approaches to Cuba with similar "decorum and dignity." Furthermore, he conveyed the impression that similar procedures might well be extended to broader agreements: "When the U.S.A. was interested in searching for an agreement to prevent illegal and piratical traffic, it knew how to go about it."[14] In fact, prior to a meeting with Pat M. Holt, Staff Director of the Senate Foreign Relations Committee (whose trip to Cuba was finally authorized by the Department of State), Castro indicated that he would willingly initiate talks with Secretary of State Kissinger if the United States lifted its trade embargo.[15]

Although inconclusive, such indications of Castro's receptivity to a sincere approach by the United States in the interest of conciliation and a resolution of differences cannot be rejected outright.

The Exile Environment

The flow of refugees to the United States from Cuba may well have ended permanently on April 6, 1973. On that date the last Cubans on the original list approved by the Havana government arrived on the "Freedom Flights" that had begun in 1965.

In the meantime, earlier Cuban exiles have attempted to reorganize an increasingly uninterested and highly fragmented Cuban exile community. Militant anti-Castro groupings, such as Alpha 66, continue to reject all dialogue with Castro. This, however, is only one current of opinion. An opposite view is taken by a Puerto Rican-based organization headed by Alberto Rodríguez Moya. This group reportedly planned a conference in Jamaica at which time negotiations were to

13. *New York Times*, December 14, 1972, p. 47.
14. *San Juan Star*, April 7, 1973, p. 12.
15. *Los Angeles Times*, July 4, 1974, p. 2. Castro said more or less the same thing to Senators Jacob K. Javits and Claiborne Pell when they visited Cuba in September 1974. (See *New York Times*, October 1, 1974, p. 6.)

take place with four "opposition" leaders from Cuba who would attend under the personal authorization of Castro himself. It was hoped such talks would lead to productive discussions between the exiles and the Castro government.

There has also been created (in Costa Rica) another exile grouping that has adopted the name "People's Revolutionary Party" (PRP). It is openly supported by such "democratic-left" leaders as ex-Costa Rican President José Figueres and Puerto Rican Arturo Morales Carrión. An officer of the organization was quoted as saying that the new party's position is that insurrection inside Cuba is the only realistic solution for opponents of Premier Castro.[16] Yet, during an exile dinner in Puerto Rico in January 1973 honoring Cuban patriot José Martí, guest speaker José Figueres surprised his audience by urging the exiles to keep their "minds open to solutions for the Cuban problem." [17] In essence, he recommended dialogue with Castro and even offered to serve as an intermediary in any possible negotiations.

While it is impossible to characterize the sentiments of the Cuban exiles as a whole, such developments only reemphasize the obvious —that the so-called exile community is so fragmented that no cohesive and sustained opposition can possibly be brought to bear against principal U. S. decision-makers if and when conciliation with Castro is deemed to be in the general U. S. interest.

The Hemispheric Environment

Cuba has become but one of many disturbing issues confronting the Organization of American States. The anti-Cuban diplomatic and commercial embargo imposed by the organization in 1964 has lost considerable moral force as a growing number of OAS members have joined Mexico in unilaterally reestablishing ties with the Castro regime. They include Peru, Argentina, Jamaica, Trinidad-Tobago, Barbados, Panama and Venezuela. Chile developed close ties with Cuba under the Allende regime; however, one of the first acts of the Chilean military junta that deposed the former legal government in September 1973 was to cut official relations with Cuba. On the other hand, Guyana, an independent hemispheric state whose membership in the OAS has not yet been accepted, has also recognized Cuba. A State Department spokesman characterized the English-speaking nations' joint decision to ignore the sanctions mandate as "an unfortunate

16. *San Juan Star*, January 18, 1973, p. 23.
17. *San Juan Star*, January 31, 1973, p. 8.

development." [18] But continued support for the embargo continues to deteriorate; Ecuador, Colombia and Nicaragua have considered restoring relations with Havana in the coming months. There was optimism that the OAS would vote to eliminate its anti-Cuban sanctions when a special foreign ministers meeting was called for this purpose in November 1974. But the resolution presented to abolish the quarantine measures failed to gain the support of the required two-thirds majority, although only three negative votes were cast —plus six abstentions, including that of the United States.[19] Thus, formally, Cuba remains an outcast within the hemisphere.

The failure to lift the 1964 sanctions and the possible readmission of Cuba to hemispheric forums outside the formal framework of the inter-American system are only symptoms of a deeper malaise within the Organization of American States. Castro has often reiterated that Cuba would not be interested in rejoining a group so heavily dominated by the United States. And, in the face of U. S. actions and policies in the area, the idea of Latin American unity directed against the paramount hemispheric power has asserted itself in recent statements and attitudes of even traditionally pro-U. S. Latin American statesmen like OAS Secretary-General Galo Plaza. What has become obvious is the incompatibility of basic interests between the United States and Latin America—particularly in the economic sphere. Deputy Premier Carlos Rafael Rodríguez of Cuba was roundly applauded at a March 1973 meeting of the United Nations-sponsored Economic Commission for Latin America (ECLA) in Quito when he said that "at the present moment in history, there is no community of interests between the United States and the rest of the hemisphere".[20]

The differences over basic economic and political issues between the United States and Latin America have become so obvious that even the United States has come to recognize officially that the structure—and perhaps even the purposes—of the hemispheric organization should be drastically modified. President Luis Echeverría of Mexico, in fact, publicly proposed the creation of a new hemispheric organization that would include Cuba but not the United States.[21] While its basic purpose would be economic—"to establish prices for Latin American raw materials and protect its marketing structure" [22] —such an alliance of Latin American countries could well lead to the

18. *New York Times*, December 14, 1972, p. 10.
19. See *New York Times*, November 13, 1974, p. 10.
20. *Latin America*, Vol. VII, No. 13 (March 30, 1973), p. 101.
21. See the *San Diego Union*, July 16, 1974, p. A1.
22. *Ibid.*

abandonment of the OAS in favor of a political organization for the region in which direct U. S. participation would be excluded. Should this be achieved, there is every possibility that Cuba might find membership in the new organization more in consonance with its own foreign and national policy objectives.

Whatever the case, the developments in these environments represent cogent indicators of forces which highly condition U. S. Cuban policy. The keyword is change. And such policy change is not likely to be resisted too far. Indeed, it is now in the interest of the United States to recognize its inevitability. Perhaps the new American president, Gerald R. Ford, will soon see the advisability of pressing forward with the onerous and intricate task of moving away from the politics of hostility toward the Cuban revolutionary regime. If so, the United States will finally advance into a new phase of its Cuban policy—that of reconciliation.

SELECTED BIBLIOGRAPHY

Books

Abel, Elie. *The Missile Crisis*. New York: Bantam Books, 1966.

Barkin, David P. and Manitzas, Rita R. (eds.). *Cuba: The Logic of the Revolution*. Andover, Mass.: Warner Modular Publications, 1973.

Bonachea, Rolando E. and Valdés, Nelson P. (eds.). *Cuba in Revolution*. Garden City, N. Y.: Anchor Books, Doubleday and Company, Inc., 1972.

Bonsal, Philip. *Cuba, Castro, and the United States*. Pittsburgh: University of Pittsburgh Press, 1971.

Boorstein, Edward. *The Economic Transformation of Cuba*. New York: Monthly Review Press, 1968.

Clissold, Stephen, Jr. (ed.). *Soviet Relations with Latin America, 1918-1968*. New York: Oxford University Press, 1970.

Debray, Regis. *Revolution in the Revolution?* New York: Monthly Review Press, 1967.

Draper, Theodore. *Castro's Revolution: Myths and Realities*. New York: Thomas and Hudson, 1962.

— *Castroism: Theory and Practice*. New York: Praeger, 1965.

Fagen, Richard R. *The Transformation of Political Culture in Cuba*. Palo Alto: Stanford University Press, 1970.

— Brody, Richard A.; O'Leary, Thomas J. *Cubans in Exile: Disaffection and Revolution*. Palo Alto: Stanford University Press, 1968.

Fort, Gilberto V. *The Cuban Revolution of Fidel Castro Viewed From Abroad: Annotated Bibliography*. Lawrence: University of Kansas Libraries, 1969.

Goldenberg, Boris. *The Cuban Revolution and Latin America*. New York: Praeger, 1965.

González, Edward. *Cuba Under Castro: The Limits of Charisma*. Boston: Houghton Mifflin Co., 1974.

Horowitz, Irving Louis. *Cuban Communism*. New York: Aldine Publishing Company, 1970.

145

11

Huberman, Leo and Sweezy, Paul M. *Socialism in Cuba.* New York: Monthly Review Press, 1969.

Jackson, D. Bruce. *Castro, the Kremlin, and Communism in Latin America.* Baltimore: The John Hopkins Press, 1969.

Karol, K. S. *The Guerrillas in Power.* New York: Hill and Wang, 1970.

Kenner, Martin and Petras, James (eds.). *Fidel Castro Speaks.* New York: Grove Press, 1969.

Langley, Lester D. *The Cuban Policy of the United States: A Brief History.* New York: John Wiley & Sons, Inc., 1968.

Lockwood, Lee. *Castro's Cuba, Cuba's Castro.* New York: MacMillan, 1967.

MacGaffey, Wyatt and Barnett, Clifford R. *Twentieth Century Cuba: Background of the Cuban Revolution.* Garden City, N. Y.: Anchor Books, Doubleday and Company, Inc., 1965.

Matthews, Herbert. *Fidel Castro.* New York: Simon and Schuster, 1969.

Mesa-Lago, Carmelo (ed.). *Revolutionary Change in Cuba.* Pittsburgh: University of Pittsburgh Press, 1971.

O'Connor, James. *The Origins of Socialism in Cuba.* Ithaca: Cornell University Press, 1969.

Plank, John (ed.). *Cuba and the United States: Long-Range Perspectives.* Washington: The Brookings Institution, 1967.

Ruiz, Ramón Eduardo. *Cuba: The Making of a Revolution.* New York: W. W. Norton & Co., 1970.

Scheer, Robert and Zeitlin, Maurice. *Cuba: An American Tragedy.* New York: Penguin Books, 1964.

Seers, Dudley (ed.). *Cuba, the Economic and Social Revolution.* Chapel Hill: University of North Carolina Press, 1964.

Suárez, Andrés. *Cuba: Castroism and Communism, 1959-1966.* Boston: M.I.T. Press, 1967.

Suchlichi, Jaime. *The Cuban Revolution: A Documentary Guide, 1952-1969.* Coral Gables: University of Miami Press, 1971.

— (ed.). *Cuba, Castro, and Revolution.* Coral Gables: University of Miami Press, 1972.

Sutherland, Elizabeth. *The Youngest Revolution.* New York: The Dial Press, Inc., 1969.

Thomas, Hugh. *Cuba: The Pursuit of Freedom.* New York: Harper & Row, 1971.

Valdés, Nelson and Lieuwen, Edwin. *The Cuban Revolution: A Research-Study Guide* (1959-1969). Albuquerque: University of New Mexico Press, 1971.

Williams, William Appleman. *The United States, Cuba, and Castro.* New York: Monthly Review Press, 1962.

Wilkerson, Loree. *Fidel Castro's Political Programs from Reformism to Marxism-Leninism.* Gainesville: University of Florida Press, 1965.

Zeitlin, Maurice. *Revolutionary Politics and the Cuban Working Class.* Princeton: Princeton University Press, 1967.

Amaro, Nelson V. "Las fases de la revolución cubana." *Aportes* (Paris), No. 13 (July 1969), pp. 81-101.

Bender, Lynn Darrell. "U. S. Cuban Policy: Subtle Modifications and the Implications of the American-Soviet 'Understandings,'" *The Journal of International and Comparative Studies* (now *Potomac Review*), Vol. 5, No. 2 (Spring 1972), pp. 50-67.

— "U. S. Cuban Policy Under the Nixon Administration: Subtle Modifications," *Revista/Review Interamericana*, Vol. II, No. 3 (Fall 1972), pp. 330-341.

— "Guantánamo: Its Political, Military and Legal Status," *Caribbean Quarterly*, Vol. 19, No. 1 (March 1973), pp. 80-86.

— "U. S. Claims Against the Cuban Government: An Obstacle to Rapprochement," *Inter-American Economic Affairs*, Vol. 27, No. 1 (Summer 1973), pp. 3-13.

— "The Cuban Exiles: An Analytical Sketch," *Journal of Latin American Studies* (London), Vol. 5, Part 2 (November 1973), pp. 271-278.

— "Gitmo: Vestige of Americana in Cuba," United States Naval Institute *Proceedings*, Vol. 99, No. 12/850 (December 1973), pp. 114-116.

"Cuba, the United States, and Sugar," *Caribbean Studies*, Vol. 14, No. 1. (April 1974).

Bonsal, Philip W. "Cuba, Castro, and the United States." *Foreign Affairs* (January 1967), pp. 260-276.

Cozeon, Jon: Drymis, Karen; Hitt, Debroah; and Arensberg, Mariada. *Cuban Guerrilla Training Centers and Radio Havana: A Selected Bibliography*. Washington: The American University Center for Research in Social Systems, 1968.

Crasswell, Robert D. *Cuba and the United States: The Tangled Relationship*. New York: Foreign Policy Association, 1971.

Fagen, Richard R. "Calculation and Emotion in Foreign Policy: The Cuban Case." *Journal of Conflict Resolution*, Vol. VI, No. 3 (September 1962), pp. 214-221.

— "Charismatic Authority and the Leadership of Fidel Castro." *Western Political Quarterly*, 18 (June 1965), pp. 275-284.

— "Mass Mobilization in Cuba: The Symbolism of Struggle." *Journal of International Affairs*, Vol. 20, No. 2 (1966), pp. 254-271.

González, Edward. "Castro's Revolution, Cuban Communist Appeals, and the Soviet Response." *World Politics*, Vol. XXI, No. 1 (October 1968), pp. 39-68.

— "Castro: The Limits of Charisma." *Problems of Communism* (July/August), 1970, pp. 12-24.

— "The United States and Castro: Breaking the Deadlock," *Foreign Affairs* (July 1972), pp. 722-737.

Johnson, Leland C. "U. S. Business Interests in Cuba and the Rise of Castro." *World Politics*, Vol. XVII, No. 3 (April 1965), pp. 440-460.

León, Luis Aguilar. "La proyección internacional de la revolución cubana." *Exilio*, 3-4 (Winter 1969 - Spring 1970), pp. 82-95.

Mesa-Lago, Carmelo. "Availability and Reliability of Statistics in Socialist Cuba." *Latin American Research Review* (Spring 1969), pp. 53-91 (Fall 1969), pp. 47-81.

Re, Edward D. "The Foreign Claims Settlement Commission and International Claims." *Syracuse Law Review*, Vol. 13, No. 4 (Summer 1962), pp. 516-526.

Tretiak, Daniel. *Cuba's Relations with the Communist System: The Politics of a Communist Independent, 1967-1970.* ASG Monograph. No. 4 Waltham, Mass.: Westinghouse Electric Corporation, Advanced Studies Group, 1971.

— "Cuba and the Soviet Union: The Growing Accommodation, 1964-65." *Orbis*, XI (Summer 1967), pp. 439-458.

Wilson, Desmond P., Jr. "Strategic Projections and Policy Options in the Soviet-Cuban Relationship." *Orbis* (Summer 1968), pp. 504-515.

Government Documents

U. S. Department of State. *U. S. Policy Toward Cuba.* Publication 7690, Inter-American Series 88, 1964.

U. S. Congress, House of Representatives. Committee on Foreign Affairs, *Claims of U. S. Nationals Against the Government of Cuba.* Hearings Before the Sub-Committee on Inter-American Affairs, Washington: Government Printing Office, 1964.

U. S. Congress. House of Representatives. Committee on Foreign Affairs. *Cuba and the Caribbean.* Hearings Before the Sub-Committee on Inter-American Affairs. Washington: Government Printing Office, 1970.

U. S. Congress. Senate. Committee on Foreign Relations. *Aircraft Hijacking Convention.* Hearing Before the Committee on Foreign Relations. Washington: Government Printing Office, 1971.

U. S. Congress. House of Representatives. Committee on Foreign Affairs. *Soviet Naval Activities in Cuba, Part 2.* Hearings Before the Sub-Committee on Inter-American Affairs. Washington: Government Printing Office, 1971.

U. S. Congress. Senate. Committee on Foreign Relations. *United States Policy Towards Cuba.* Hearing Before the Committee on Foreign Relations. Washington: Government Printing Office, 1971.

INDEX

Mikoyan, Anastas, 20.
Miró Cardona, José, 15.
Missile Crisis (1962), 14, 24-25, 54, 60, 66-67, 118, 129.
Mississippi River, 113.
Moa Bay Mining Company, 103, 107.
Monroe Doctrine, 26 n, 36.
Moorer, Thomas A., 61 n.
Moral Incentives, 54.
Morales Carrión, Arturo, 141.

National Liberation Action, 40.
Nationalizations.
See Cuba, Expropiations and Nationalizations.
Nicaragua, 16.
Nixon, Richard M., 16, 20, 22, 33-34, 43, 71-72, 82 n, 84-86, 122, 130, 137, 138.
Nixon Administration, 31, 34, 36-37, 44, 82 n. 84 n, 86, 139.
North American Sugar Industries, 107.

O'Connor, James, 14 n.
Oil, 21, 97.
Olcott, Charles S., 4 n.
O'Leary, Jeremiah, 90.
O'Leary, Thomas J., 49 n.
Organization of American States (OAS), 24, 27, 30, 32, 56, 83-91, 129, 134-136, 141-143.
Expulsion of Cuba, 23-24.
Foreign Ministers Meetings, 22-23, 27-28.
General Assemblies, 90, 126 n.
Inter-American Peace Committee, 21.
Sanctions Against Cuba, 27-37, 57 n, 128-131, 134, 136, 141-142.
Osborne, John, 86 n.
Osgood, C. E., 85 n.
Ostend Manifesto, 4.
Oswald, J. Gregory, 62 n.

Panama, 16, 57 n, 113, 114, 115-116, 136, 141.
Panama Canal, 3, 113, 114, 115 n, 116.

Pazos Vea, Javier Felipe, 123 n, 124 n.
Pell, Claiborne, 140 n.
Peoples' Republic of China.
See China, Communist.
Peoples' Revolutionary Party (Partido Revolucionario del Pueblo-PRP), 141.
Peru, 56, 57 n, 76, 99, 136, 141.
Petras, James, 20 n, 24 n, 34 n, 64 n, 110 n, 112 n.
Phillippines, 98.
Phillips, R. Hart, 111 n.
Plank, John, 14 n, 126 n.
Platt, Orville, 5.
Plaza, Galo, 142.
Poland, 101, 109.
Political Isolation.
See Cuba.
Polk, James, 4.
Popular Socialist Party (Partido Socialista Popular-PSP), 51-53.
Portell Vilá, Herminio, 2 n.
Prado, Manuel, 99.
Puerto Rico, 97, 114, 116 n, 117, 122, 140.

Re, Edward D., 102 n, 103 n, 105 n.
Rebus Sic Stantibus, 116.
Revolutionary Communist Union (Unión Revolucionaria Comunista-URC), 51 n.
Río Treaty (1947), 26 n, 27.
Rivers, Mendel, 69.
Rodríguez, Carlos Rafael, 50, 52 n, 55 n, 142.
Rodríguez Moya, Alberto, 141.
Rogers, William P., 84 n, 126 n, 138.
Roosevelt, Franklin D., 5.
Roosevelt Roads Naval Base, 114.
Ruiz, Ramón Eduardo, 2 n.
Rusk, Dean, 67, 77 n.

Sanctions Against Cuba.
See Organizations of American States, Sanctions Against Cuba.
Sauzier, A. Guy, 96 n.

153

lution (Partido Unido de la Revolución Socialista-PURS), 51 n.
United States.
Central Intelligence Agency (CIA),
16, 122.
Congress, 20, 25, 69, 98, 102 n, 104,
120, 122, 138, 140.
Congressional Hearings, 30 n, 32 n,
36 n, 37 n, 38 n, 39 n, 40 n, 42 n,
43 n, 62 n, 68 n, 69 n, 82 n, 91 n,
96 n, 98 n, 99 n, 100 n, 102 n, 103 n,
104 n, 110 n, 115 n, 119 n, 120 n,
121 n, 126 n, 127 n.
Cuban Assets Control Regulations
(1963), 105.
Cuban Claims Program.
See U.S. Foreign Claims Settlement Commission.
Defense Intelligence Agency
(DIA), 39 n, 91 n.
Department of Commerce, 6, 55 n,
94 n.
Department of Defense, 68.
Department of Health, Education
and Welfare.
See Cuban Refugee Program.
Department of State, 16, 19 n, 21,
25 n, 27 n, 28 n, 29 n, 30, 36 n,
37, 64, 67, 71, 83, 95 n, 99, 105,
112-113, 117, 119 n, 120, 140.
Department of the Treasury, 105.
Efforts to Overthrow Castro, 10,
16, 19, 20-23, 27-31, 35-41, 59, 87,
91, 111-112, 120, 122-124, 125-127,
128-130.
Foreign Claims Settlement Com-
mission (FCSC), 105-107, 107 n,
109 n.
Foreign Policy Decision-Making,
79, 83.
Geopolitical Relation to Cuba,
2-4.
Interest in the Caribbean.
See Caribbean, U.S. Interest in.
Interest in Latin America.
See Latin America, United States
Interest in.

International Claims Commission,
105 n.
International Claims Settlement
Act of 1949, 104, 105 n.
Intervention in Cuba.
See Cuba, U.S. Intervention in.
Intervention in the Dominican Re-
public, 17, 26 n, 29.
Intervention in Guatemala, 16, 18.
Investments in Cuba, 6, 21, 101,
110.
Jones-Costigan Act, 98.
Military, 113-114.
National Security, 2, 113.
National Security Council (NSC),
82, 86.
Navy, 112-114.
Regional Relationships, 89-92.
Strategic Interests, 3, 90, 113-114.
Sugar Quota.
See Sugar.
Surveillance of Cuba, 24, 33, 42,
67.
War Claims Act of 1948, 105 n.
War Claims Commission, 105 n.
Western Hemisphere Policy.
See Western Hemisphere, Unit-
ed States Policy.
United States-Communist China Re-
lations, 34, 44, 83-87, 93, 139.
United States-Cuban Relations, 76-
78, 87-89, 125.
Accomodative Policy, 78, 89, 128,
130-136.
Claims, 6, 30, 93, 101-110, 130, 134.
Claims, Pre-Settlement Adjudicat-
ion of, 104.
Containment Policy, 10, 23-26, 37,
42, 44, 76, 78, 89, 103, 125, 129-
130, 136.
Dialectic of Hostility, 14.
Diplomatic Relations, 14, 18, 22,
99, 118, 130, 133, 138-139.
Economic Relations, 4, 6-7, 14, 17,
26, 97-101, 112, 130, 133-136, 138.
Efforts Toward Accomodation, 15-
18, 26, 34, 42-44, 77-78, 85.

079027